In **I Play to Win**, Stan Mikita, an aggressive competitor and outstanding member of the **Chicago Black Hawks**, has written a book rich in hockey lore, anecdotes, and insights into the game.

For young players and hockey fans he explains the difference between rough hockey and mean hockey, and how a player learns to adjust his style of play to his own capabilities and the special skills or shortcomings of his opponents.

But for Czechoslovakian-born **Stan Mikita**, hockey is more than a sport and an exciting way to make a living: It is an expression of the North American way of life—the will to win.

I PLAY TO WIN was originally published by William Morrow and Company, Inc.

I PLAY TO WIN

Stan Mikita

A POCKET BOOK EDITION published by
Simon & Schuster of Canada, Ltd. • Richmond Hill, Ontario, Canada
Registered User of the Trademark

I PLAY TO WIN

Morrow edition published December, 1969

Pocket Book edition published November, 1970

2nd printing......September, 1970

This *Pocket Book* edition includes every word contained in the original, higher-priced edition. It is printed from brand-new plates made from completely reset, clear, easy-to-read type. Trademarks registered in the United States and other countries.

Standard Book Number: 671-75632-X.
Library of Congress Catalog Card Number: 73-95308.
Copyright, ©, 1969, by Stan Mikita. All rights reserved. This *Pocket Book* edition is published by arrangement with William Morrow & Company, Inc.

Printed in Canada.

To my parents, the Mikitas
and the Gvoths, in whom
I have been twice blessed.

Contents

Illustrations follow page 82

	INTRODUCTION	ix
	AUTHOR'S NOTE	xi
1	The Game Starts in the Morning	1
2	The Gift of a Child	13
3	A "DP" Tries Harder ... He Has To	22
4	The Rink Rats	31
5	The Link Is Formed	40
6	Up to the Black Hawks	52
7	It Pays to Win	60
8	*Le Petit Diable*	70
9	Tricks of the Trade	78
10	Champions	85
11	Bobby and I	93
12	Who's Hurting?	101
13	Collecting Silverware	111
14	The Hired Hand	119
15	A Man's Family	126
16	Back Home Again	133
17	It's Worth Trying	142
18	Me a Vice-President?	153
19	Friends, Fans, and Phonies	160
20	Who's No. 2?	169

Introduction

Often when people ask me about Stan I say, "Well, he's the worst center I've had on my line for the last ten years," and it takes them a moment to catch on that he's the only center I've had in that time.

Seriously, nobody is in a better position than I am to appreciate just how good a hockey player Stan Mikita is. But I don't have to tell anybody about Stan's ability on the ice, the record speaks for itself.

Just as important are his qualities as a man and teammate. I know that the youngsters who admire him and hope to pattern themselves after him as a hockey player will benefit from reading the story of his life. As a close friend, I know just how devoted Stan is to hockey and to the youngsters who will follow in his skates, and I'm certain that in this book, as on the ice, he has given 100% of his ability.

KENNY WHARRAM

Author's Note

Personal friends and associates in hockey for several years now have urged me to write the story of my life in full. They thought I had an interesting story to tell and impressed on me that rather than writing the customary "how to do it" book or superficial story, I should concentrate on a real autobiography. I was a little reluctant to write about my life at first, but the more I thought about it, the more enthusiastic I became, because it did seem to me my story was a little different from that of the average athlete.

It isn't part of my aim to set the record straight on how I decided to switch from being what people considered an over-aggressive player to being thought worthy of the Lady Byng Trophy for sportsmanship. I don't feel I have to put it down in writing to let people know that I've changed a little bit—and maybe I really haven't changed all that much, even though I have considerably reduced the penalty minutes.

Although this isn't intended to be an instructional book, I hope it will help youngsters to play the game by explaining how I do it and how I improved my skills as I went along. If youngsters derive a benefit from the parts of the book that deal with hockey techniques, that makes it just that much more worthwhile and gratifying to me.

Many people have helped me get all this on paper but the ideas are all my own. I thank them for their hard work and any success I may have had in telling the story of my life just the way it happened.

STAN MIKITA

I PLAY TO WIN

1

The Game Starts in the Morning

THIS IS the day of the game, Wednesday, March 26, 1969, and we are playing the New York Rangers at the Chicago Stadium tonight. We call it a "nothing" game because the Black Hawks are firmly locked in sixth place, as unbelievable as it is, and the Rangers are sure of making the playoffs. But there are no "nothing" games for me, I still want to—need to—win any game I play in.

Usually the kids, Meg and Scott, come into our bedroom at 9 A.M., but Jill makes sure they don't come in until a quarter to ten this morning. I'm awake a little earlier than that and I see the seven-week-old baby, Jane Elizabeth, smiling at me. Jill has placed her canvas-backed reclining chair on the bed and she's been watching me sleep.

I get up, wash without shaving (I never shave before a game because the sweat and cold air hitting my face will irritate it) and have black coffee, which is all I ever take in the morning. While I'm watching "Andy of Mayberry" on TV with the kids, the phone rings and it's Jill's uncle. A friend of his, a judge from Wheaton, wonders if he can bring three kids down to the bench before the game to meet me and Pit Martin. I say, "Fine, come down during the warm-up."

The team meeting's set for 11 A.M. at the stadium, so I leave the house at 10:30 as it doesn't take more than half an hour to drive from Elmhurst. Most of the team are in the dressing room already and Coach Billy Reay sends Assistant Trainer Don (Socko) Uren up to call the players who are taking a skate. (We never have a regular workout on the day of a game, and the meeting is more to count heads and break up

1

the day so a fellow doesn't plan some other all-day activity that'll take his mind off the game.)

"There's not much I can tell you now," says Reay, "other than to remember not to disgrace yourselves. I know you've got nothing really to gain but the people out there are paying good money to see us and it's up to you to provide them with entertainment." And as an afterthought he added, "Don't forget the beer party Monday after it's all over."

Everybody snickers, probably because we'd rather be winners and have champagne. Nobody wants to go out a loser and you still wish you had a mathematical chance for the playoffs; but it's too late to think about that. In a way it's a relief to get the season over with even if there's not much cause for celebration.

I start checking my equipment. I look at the skates to see how much hollow I have in the blades. I like a deep hollow because it gives me two edges to skate on and to dig in for sudden stops. With two edges, I can stop different ways in various situations. Yes, trainer Nick Garen's done a good job. He's kept about two or three inches flat, in the middle of the blade, a bit more than most players use. I've had these blades only two or three weeks, and they're just right. The laces are fine. I don't have to check the pads or the uniform since Socko Uren takes care of that and I can depend on him.

I walk over into the other room to check my sticks. I like to have at least five ready for each game. There are five here from last Sunday's game, but one of them is starting to crack and the blade's wobbly. Another one is chipping in the handle, it won't last too long so I'd better put it aside. That leaves three sticks all made up. I ask Uren if the new sticks have arrived yet, and he says they're supposed to get here about 1:30. I'll have to fix them up tonight, before the game, because I've got to go home now for the pre-game meal.

On my way out of the stadium I run into Rod Gilbert of the Rangers. They've had their pre-game meeting, too. We exchange a few words about what a peculiar season it has been in so many ways. Rod wonders if Christian Bros., a stick manufacturer I just became connected with, could make up a dozen of his model for him to try out. I say they're making up samples for me, too, and we'd be glad to make some sticks for him.

On the way home I stop at Fred's Meat Market on the

The Game Starts in the Morning / 3

northwest side of Chicago for half a dozen steaks. I get home about 1:30. Jill has turned on the outdoor gas barbecue and I begin cooking the steaks. I like to watch them myself because I like them rare, almost raw, and so do the kids. Jill likes hers medium well done and neither the kids nor I would touch hers with a ten-foot pole. (A steak dinner about this time the day of the game is the usual routine for a hockey player. Of course, on the road the team eats as a group.)

After giving Jill a hand with clearing the table and trying to soothe the baby, who's a little cranky, I go upstairs about 2 P.M. for a nap with the kids. (A one- to two-hour nap after lunch is also a standard training procedure on the day of the game, at home or on the road, and most of the players have no trouble falling asleep, it's such a habit.) I have to holler a little at Meg and Scott to get them to stop playing, and we're asleep in fifteen minutes. I get up about 4:30 and the phone rings. It's Kenny Wharram and he asks if Jill's going to the game. She misses only a few games each year but has been staying at home more lately because of the baby. She says yes, which means Kenny will pick me up and we'll drive down together and Jill will pick up his wife Jeanie a little later.

At a quarter to five the doorbell rings. Jill answers it and it's a boy selling subscriptions to one of the two Chicago evening newspapers. Jill tells the boy we take the other paper but he leaves a sample copy anyway. I turn to the sports section. It's strange the kid should bring the paper today because there's a headline, "Mikita Not on Block, Says Reay." It's nice to hear that coming from the coach and I hope he does have quite a bit to say about trades because he's the guy who has to handle the men. All year long I've been hearing stories about trades and my name has been mentioned most often. I've half been expecting to be traded but I hope Reay is right and I won't be.

Kenny arrives at five and we drive the regular route to the Stadium, down the Eisenhower Expressway, off at Paulina, then a few blocks over. Earlier in the season, if things are going bad, we might switch routes just to change our luck, but now it doesn't matter. We listen to the radio, then Kenny says, "You figure we'll be playing against the Ratelle line?"

"Yeah, that's what I've been thinking," I say. "We've got to try and stop them. Remember how Ratelle busted through last time they were here?"

"When they're out there, we've usually got to watch them,"

says Kenny. "If we're skating right, let's make them watch us. If we're skating, we won't have to worry about them because they'll have their hands full trying to check us and then everything will fall into place."

"That's right, that's the way we'll play it," I say.

"You know something," he says, "Kenny Jr."—he's thirteen—"told Jeanie the other day, 'Gee, Daddy needs only three more goals for 250. Won't that be something?' So Jeanie later said to me, 'You only need five more goals to reach your bonus, isn't that right?' And I said, 'Well, we've only got three games to go.' She just said, 'Well, all you need is two tonight, two on Saturday, and one on Sunday. And all you need is three for 250.' Isn't that something?"

Kenny was surprised because Jeanie never talks about hockey, but it gets me thinking. He has twenty-five goals now and needs five more for a bonus, maybe we can get it for him. Goals and points don't mean anything from a bonus standpoint to me because that's not the kind of contract I have. But I've got twenty-seven goals and sixty-two assists for eighty-nine points, the second-highest total I've ever had, and if that's a bad season like some guys have been writing, I don't know what a good one is. Of course, the points alone don't mean that much to me if the team isn't going anywhere.

So I tell Kenny, "Well, maybe Jeanie's right and you can do it. Just try and get in the clear and I'll try and get the puck over to you."

We pick up cups of coffee at a vendor's stand inside the stadium and when we get down to the dressing room I strip to my pants and shoes and go to the stick rack to see if my sticks have arrived. There are half a dozen new ones. I pick up the first one and flex it but it's too whippy. With the slap shot a whippy stick's likely to break a lot easier in the handle or down in the neck. I pick up another stick and it's not too good. I give them a good test by leaning hard on the handle while holding the stick in regular fashion, figuring if they don't break while I'm trying them out they'll stand up better in the game. I break the third one, then the fourth. The next two also break and out of six I've got nothing. (This testing is standard for me and the other players. I normally reject half to three-fourths of all the sticks for one reason or another. They've got to feel absolutely right and most of us are as fussy about our sticks as women are about their hair.)

The Game Starts in the Morning / 5

Socko tells me that Bob Schmautz likes the same kind I do, so why don't I try those. I take three and I like them. I have Don tape up the end of the handles for me with black tape, then I finish them off with white tape so my glove palms will last longer. I like the handles tubular, almost like a bike handle, and without a knob.

By twenty minutes to seven I'm all dressed except for my shoulder pads and jersey. I take the sticks out and machine down the bottom of the blade. (This affects the "lie" of the stick, or the angle the handle makes with the blade when it rests on the ice.) Some days I like the handle resting low, today I want it high, more up and down. When I'm finished with that it's time to tighten the skates, pull on my jersey and put vaseline on my face for protection from the cold, and as I wipe off the excess Coach Reay comes in and says, "Okay, let's have a good warm-up now."

The Stadium is starting to fill up at 7 P.M. and the judge from Wheaton, the man Jill's uncle called about, is waiting near the bench with three kids. I sneak them in the back of the bench and get the players to come over and sign autographs. They leave and I warm up, taking a few shots, and one of Schmautz's sticks doesn't feel too good so I discard it. I'll use two of his and the three I have left from Sunday.

We go down to the dressing room after the warm-up and I'm a little nervous, get the dry heaves. I've been trying all day not to think about the game, but now in the final fifteen minutes before it starts at 7:30 I give myself time to concentrate on it. I sort of put myself in a trance, and I'm not kidding.

When the warning buzzer to go up sounds, we start filing up the steps, coming out on the ice, and the roar of the crowd still moves me after more than ten years. I head for the bench and the game starts, with Pit Martin's line—Dennis Hull at left wing, Jim Pappin at right wing—on the ice. The Rangers have the Ratelle line out there, which surprises me.

Martin's line is out there for more than two minutes, which is a long time for a first shift. I'm surprised Reay leaves them out there that long. Then Andre Boudrias, Bobby Hull and Chico Maki come out for us against New York's Larry Jeffrey, Don Marshall and Ron Stewart. They're also out there two minutes and I'm waiting impatiently with Wharram and Gilles Marotte, who has been our left wing the last three games. First the Martin line, then the Hull line hems the Rangers in their end, but they're out there too long. Sure, when you've got them going you have a tendency to stay out there longer, but by the same token when you're out too long you get winded and that's when they break away and score a goal on you. It almost happens, as Dave Balon of the Rangers looks like he's home free from the red line, but fortunately it's called offside.

Finally, my lines goes out there, two minutes later than normally. The first shift is very important to a hockey player. He likes to go out there maybe from forty seconds to a full minute, then get off while the other guys come on. We should have been out there at the two-minute mark, but now it's past four minutes of the period. We find the Rangers have changed strategy on us, using the line centered by Walt Tkaczuk, with Balon at left wing and Bob Nevin at right wing. It's a checking line, the one they use against a hot line, which maybe we are again. I know that a few games ago my back stopped bothering me and I took off the brace and started moving better.

We're in their end and I'm behind the net. The puck goes out to our young defenseman Ray McKay, standing near the blue line, and he's got a clear shot. I decide I'd better go out front and screen his shot or deflect it. He lets a shot go along the ice and all I do is turn my stick a bit and the puck goes between Ranger goalie Eddie Giacomin's legs.

The public announcer tells the crowd, "Goal scored by Ray McKay for the first National League goal of his career," and a great roar goes up. Giacomin and I catch each other's eyes, and he throws back his head in surprise and takes off a glove, pointing at me, and I nod my head, yes, but wonder what am I going to do about it. I could let the kid have the goal. I've been here ten years and I've never stolen a goal yet. There's a stoppage of play and McKay comes over and asks, "You tipped in that goal, didn't you?" He goes over to the officials and tells them. The correction is made over the loudspeaker and a boo goes up from the crowd.

I'm stunned! This is the first time since I've played hockey that I've scored a goal and been booed for it on home ice. My first reaction is what in hell do you have to do to please these people, but I realize it stems back to a lot of games and the fact we're in sixth place. And McKay has been playing well and really trying hard, and the crowd is pulling for him to make good.

Play continues, first one line then the other, and we can

sense we're all skating tonight and that we want this game more than the Rangers do. The crowd is waiting for Bobby Hull to score. He already has broken his record of fifty-four goals in a season by one, but they're eager to have him reach sixty, so every time he even touches the puck a roar goes up.

Jim Neilson of the Rangers is in the penalty box and we've got a power play going as I hit the ice for the third time. I'm facing off with Balon in their end and I get the puck back to Bobby at right point, but Giacomin turns aside his shot and the puck goes into a corner where I'm tied up against the boards. I squirm loose enough to kick the puck to Whitey Stapleton at left point. He whips it across to Bobby, who winds up like he's going to slap, then slides it to Kenny after drawing the defenseman. Kenny's open on the right side and by this time I'm in front and to the left of the net.

Kenny sees me, I don't even have to yell, but he plays it too easily. If he'd let me have it right away Giacomin wouldn't even have gotten a stick on the puck, but Kenny decides to take just one more stride, then throws the puck across. Giacomin pops it in the air with his stick, but then he's out of the play and Marotte skates in and puts the puck into the open net. We're ahead 2–0.

The period is almost over and Bobby still hasn't got the goal, although he's had a couple of good chances. This time he gets himself in a good spot, nobody checking him, cruising in on the net while Boudrias is fishing the puck away from a couple of Rangers along the boards. Boudrias throws the puck to Bobby, who doesn't get all of it, just wobbling it toward Giacomin. But Giacomin had stopped two hard ones from Bobby earlier and he must be expecting another, for he straightens up and by the time he gets sight of the puck it goes past him.

It's 3–0, but what drives the crowd wild is that it's Bobby's 56th goal. They litter the ice with debris, but it's quickly cleared and the period is over. We go down to the locker room feeling pretty good.

I retape my stick and have a drink. Then, as usual, I rest on the bench by my cubicle, where I change and keep my clothes. We joke around a bit and I talk over a few things about the game with Kenny, whose spot is right next to mine. Billy Reay is in his private office with the door closed this night. (Sometimes he'll spend time in the dressing room talking to us, usually if things haven't gone too well, or he might call a player or two into the office for a private chat.) With two minutes to go before the second period, Reay comes into the dressing room: "All right, you're playing pretty well. Just tighten up a little more."

When we go on the ice I see Jim Neilson and I skate over. In the first period I had put the puck through his legs and I had my stick too close to him as I tried to go around his body. I caught him in the nose with the stick and now I want to tell him it was an accident. I'd never hit a player in the head purposely—well, maybe once or twice—but Neilson in particular I didn't want to do that to. He's a good player and a good guy.

"You know, that was an accident," I say. "I didn't mean to hit you."

"I know," Neilson says. "I can't seem to keep this big nose out of the way."

Later in the period, as I'm skating by I say: "Gee, you do have a big nose."

"How the hell do you think I got it?" he says. "From guys like you hitting it."

But that's later. Right now I'm hardly on the bench when I see Ratelle cutting in on our goalie Dave Dryden and whacking one past him at just twenty-six seconds of the period. That makes it 3–1, still nothing to worry about, but a little different than a three-goal lead.

My line got out on the ice a lot faster this period, just a little past two minutes, and pretty soon I'm shoving around for the puck on their end boards. A Ranger has me tied up and the puck is bouncing around, but finally I knock it down. I still don't know what to do with it, then I hear Kenny's familiar voice, "Kita! Kita!" and I guess he's about twenty feet up the slot in front of the net. I don't know exactly where he is but when you play with a guy ten years you can throw it out blind and there's a good chance he'll be in the right spot. The puck is flopping around on my stick but I get good wood on it, and pass it out hard. I'm waiting for Kenny to shoot, but he gets it away so quickly I don't see it and I think he has missed the net when all of a sudden I see the puck bouncing out and the red light going on. That makes it 4–1.

Then the Rangers turn around and get a cheap goal that ordinarily would give them a lift, if it wasn't that this game doesn't mean that much. Tkaczuk snaps the puck out from

The Game Starts in the Morning / 9

behind our net and it hits Stapleton in the rear and bounces past Dryden and the left post.

Near the end of the period Chico Maki gets a breakaway, nobody's anywhere near him, but he skates into a bad position. He has a straight road from center ice into the net, but he veers off to the right, putting himself at a bad angle and Giacomin knows Chico can't beat him with a shot, he has to try to pull him out. Giacomin comes out just to cut off the angle, then begins backing into the net, then throws out his legs and swings his stick at the puck, knocking it out of Chico's control. By the time Chico regains it he's behind the net. If Maki had come right in at Giacomin he would have had two sides to shoot at whereas this way he had only one, but on the ice you haven't got much time to think about those things.

We go down for the second intermission, leading 4–2, and Stapleton goes over to Dryden.

"Gee, I'm sorry Dave," says Whitey. "It was a bad play on my part."

"It wasn't your fault, it was mine," says Dryden. "I should have been hugging that post," which he should have but you don't think quite as sharply out there at times as you should. Anyway, it's honest of Dave to take the blame for the goal.

The second time we're on the ice this third period I face off against Tkaczuk at Dryden's right. This is a real defensive maneuver. If I can get the puck back to our defenseman then we've got possession and we're almost out of trouble, although we've still got to get it across the blue line. If we lose the draw, with the game 4–2, and Tkaczuk gets it back to the point man, their right winger will move in for a tip shot, the left winger will stay back a little to give him an out in case he can't shoot it. But I win the draw and we start moving the puck.

Marotte's playing left wing for only the fourth game and Reay has been harping on him to play up and down, just play his position and if we get possession, get up halfway between our goal line and the blue line along the boards where he'll open. Gilly does that and a defenseman throws the puck to him.

I give Gilly a yell and he gets the puck to me with a half push, almost without getting possession, and we've got a two-on-two situation opening up. I'm at center ice, halfway between the boards, about at our blue line, where you see a lot of centers take a little turn, then go almost at full speed up ice.

I try to have my wingers hit me at a time when I'm almost at half speed so I have a chance to look and if I see daylight then I turn it on. That's what I do now, go as fast as I can, then slow down just before I hit the defense. If I'm going to go through I pick up a little more speed, if I'm not, I've got to look around. This time I try to crowd the defenseman on my side toward the one that's checking Kenny, busting in on the right. I fake a shot, bring the puck back, fake a pass, fake another shot, then give it to Kenny who doesn't have it more than a split second then fires and Giacomin is off balance. He isn't sure whether I'm going to shoot or Kenny, and it goes through his legs.

As they announce the goal I go up to the penalty box and tell the official this is Kenny's 249th and the next will be 250, which will put him in a pretty exclusive group. I want him to announce it because I think Kenny ought to get a little more applause than he's getting, but he just tells the crowd it's Wharram's second goal of the night. So I ask him to announce it as No. 250 if Kenny gets a three-goal hat trick.

We think it's all over, the score 5–2, but Ratelle again comes in on the right side, Stapleton riding him, and gets off a great shot that goes past Dryden.

Dougie Jarrett is sitting on the bench next to me and he says: "Look at that son of a gun. He was off balance, he was ready to fall down and he gave Stapleton a helluva shift and got the shot off." Stapleton thought he was off balance too, that there was no way he could get back in stride, but this is the way Ratelle played. He looked like he was falling down half the time, but this was one of his decoy moves and you had to keep your mind on him every time he had the puck because he had so many moves.

We get it back in a hurry. One of our defensemen gets the puck up to Marotte and as soon as he gets the puck a Ranger rushes at him, but I'm yelling and he sees me. He throws a little, soft lob pass right over the Ranger's stick and it lands right on my blade. I turn away from Marotte toward their end and I see their defensemen up and Bobby Hull starting to bust. Instead of handling the puck, I just shovel it, like a deflection, and their defenseman is running at me, which takes him out of the play, creating a two-on-one situation. Bobby controls the puck for maybe three strides, gets over the blue line, notices the other defenseman, their last guy, coming at him, and rifles it over to Kenny busting in on the right. Kenny puts it in the net on the short side, from a difficult angle, and I go crazy. I'm so happy for the guy I want to throw him on my back and carry him around the rink, but he's gone before I can grab him.

It's a hat trick for Kenny and his 250th goal and he's just two goals away from his bonus with two games left. We've got the game put away, even though Nevin does score another goal to make it 6–4, but that's it and we win. Under happier circumstances it would have been a satisfying win for us, but this is a nothing game, although it's nice to win it. It also means something to Kenny and it means something to me because of Kenny. It also means something to us because of the way Marotte played. Now if we're all back on one line next year we're going to play the same way. Kenny and I have to be the two guys that handle the puck most of the time and Marotte's going to be the guy to do the heavy work. He's going to have to bring the puck out of our end at least part of the way and pass it to the man on the move, because that's our style, always moving.

I'm proud of the game afterwards. I'm on the ice for five of our goals, I've got a goal and three assists and they didn't score while I was out there. That's the idea of the game. Score if you can but make sure the other team doesn't. But the points are nice, too, and now I've got 93, with 28 goals and 65 assists, which is my second-best total, four short of the 97 I had in 1966–67.

I'm feeling pretty good in the dressing room and the newspapermen crowd around me.

"What did you think of the booing when you scored that goal?" asked a writer.

"I was stunned, I couldn't believe it," I say. "This is the first time since I've been playing hockey where I've seen a guy score in his own rink and be booed."

A New York writer asks: "Well, a lot of people are saying you're having a bad season. Does it seem like that to you?"

"Well, I'd like to have a bad season like this every year—93 points," I say. "I bet 100% of the forwards in the league would like to have a bad season like this, too. And it depends on who you talk to, who you ask if Mikita's having a good or bad season. If they don't like you, they say you're having a bad season. If they like you, they point out this is your second-best season so far."

I guess everybody's satisfied with my answer because pretty soon I'm free to finish dressing and meet Jill. We're going to a party that Paul Gardini, who has been opening the gate at the bench for forty-three years, is throwing. Paul likes to hold a party for the boys every year where he cooks all the food, and we've been kidding him all evening about not being able to come. But I wouldn't want to miss it and I know the food is going to taste just that much better this evening. Winning always tastes good, no matter if it's a "nothing" game.

And we've got Kenny well on his way to a bonus. Maybe Jeanie has a pipeline to the top.

(She must have, because Kenny got two more goals in the final game of the season to reach thirty goals and his bonus. I also got two goals in that wild 9–5 defeat of Detroit, in which Pit Martin got four for us and Bobby rounded out the season with No. 58. My two gave me thirty for the season and I also got assists on Kenny's goals to wind up with ninety-seven points, tying my career high. So Mikita had a bad season!)

And maybe I've got a pipeline to the top, too. Sometimes I think so, for who could have imagined this when it all started for me a long time ago and in another country?

2

The Gift of a Child

AFTER OUR first child, Meg, was born, I used to steal into her room and watch her sleep in the crib. One thought entered my mind: how could a parent give up a child? How could you bear to part with somebody whom you had helped to create, who was forever a part of you?

There are times when I still think about that, perhaps at those moments when I am happiest with my children. I can't help wondering about how my parents gave me up after raising me for eight years, to let me leave home for a new life in a country that was so far away it wasn't certain when they would see me again.

I don't want anyone to think that I'm blaming my parents or accusing them of having been cold-hearted. Far from it. I bless them for what they did. Now I'm an adult, I can understand that it was for my own good that my parents let my uncle and aunt take me from that little village in Czechoslovakia to a different, more promising kind of life in Canada.

Yet I still have to wonder. There would have to be more love than you really can express in words for a parent to do that. I don't think I could do it, as much as I love my children. But if worse came to worst, perhaps I'd do the same thing my mother and father did, no matter how much it hurt, or how much anguish there would be.

The first thing that my mother and father said to me when I returned for a visit to the old country in 1960, twelve years after I had left them, was: "Are you mad at us? Do you resent the fact that we gave you up, even if it wasn't to a stranger but to a member of the family?"

I reassured them. No matter what I said I couldn't thank them enough for the opportunity they gave me. If things had turned out differently, I don't know. Perhaps I would have resented, even hated them. If I had ended up in jail, which I could have just as easily if it weren't for hockey, I might have felt differently toward my parents. It was hockey that opened up the world to me and I owe it everything I have. It seems to me that if it hadn't been for the courage of my parents, their genuine love, nothing that I've been able to accomplish would have been possible.

I don't pretend to know what has made me the kind of person that I am. I'm not a psychiatrist or psychologist but a hockey player. I only know what I feel and think and will leave it to someone better qualified to interpret why I act the way I do and why I am the way I am. All I can do is tell the story of my life and hope that will help explain what sort of man Stan Mikita is and how he got that way. Or how Stanislav Gvoth got that way, because that was my name before my uncle Joe Mikita adopted me.

I was born May 20, 1940, in Sokolce, a village of about 500 people near the Tatra Mountains in the eastern section of Czechoslovakia. My father, George, was a maintenance man at a textile factory in Ruzomberok, the nearest town of any size. I don't remember too much of him when I was small. He would get up early in the morning, ride a motor bike to the station in the next village, and take a commuter train to Ruzomberok. Early in the afternoon he would be back and then go out and work in the fields. My mother, Emelia, also worked in the fields. It was just a farming area and nobody was rich. All we owned were little patches of land here and there. Altogether, they didn't amount to more than would make up the surface of a hockey rink. We raised potatoes, vegetables and wheat for our bread. We gave half of the wheat to the government, and what we kept just tided us by.

I didn't know that we were poor. I couldn't have told you what it meant to be rich. We lived in a big, ugly, one-story building that had been divided into housing for four families, with maybe eighteen to twenty people living in a place that altogether wasn't much larger than an average ranch house. There were four of us in the family then, my brother George being almost three years older than I. We lived in two rooms, the smaller one being a sort of kitchen where we ate in the winter and the other being the room we used for sleeping, sitting around, entertaining, and just about everything. Then there were the barn, where we kept a horse, a cow, a couple of pigs and chickens and geese, and a beat-up old shed near the

The Gift of a Child / 15

barn in which there was a wood stove my mother cooked on. We'd eat breakfast and lunch in that shed, if it was warm, but it was smelly and full of flies.

It was so different a way of life that living as I do now I find it hard to believe I was ever a part of it. I remember my mother and the other women every other day going down the steps into the stream that ran in back of our house to wash the clothes, rubbing them on rocks. They didn't even know what a washboard was. There was no indoor plumbing, and giving me a bath was a job for my mother. She had to take water from the pump outside, heat it over the wood stove, and fill up a tub. That was in the winter. In the summer, it was easier. We just took off our clothes and jumped in the stream.

There was a lot of fun, too, though. With three or four kids of my age that I chummed around with I mostly played marbles and mumbledy-peg. Behind our house was another stream that ran between the woods and the next village. It was a little thing, maybe three or four feet wide. We'd go fishing there, if you could call it fishing. We had no poles, just tried to catch the fish with our bare hands. We did catch small crabs and get one of the bigger boys to build a fire and throw the crabs in live and we'd eat them when they were cooked.

It wasn't a rough bunch. Maybe we'd throw rocks or horse turds once in a while, but we never had any gang fights that I can remember or fought more than average youngsters do anywhere.

We played a lot of soccer. That was the big thing there, although hockey's now also very popular. Either we'd be in the schoolyard kicking around a beat-up old soccer ball or we'd go to the regulation soccer field, where they had matches every Sunday afternoon, and play there. It was strictly a kids' get-up game, like we see kids playing baseball or street hockey here.

The stream would freeze over in the wintertime. I remember having a pair of screw-on skates, the old-fashioned kind with a turned-up toe like a ram's horn. I wish I had saved them. I don't know when I started skating on them, maybe I was six or seven. We saw the older kids playing a sort of shinny, so we broke limbs off the trees and shaped them into a sort of hockey stick. Most of the kids carried knives for cutting wood and whittling. Surprisingly, none of the kids used them for cutting up each other. Then we'd find an "all-purpose" horse turd or something and knock it around on the ice. I guess I fell through the ice once in a while. My mother tells me the neighbors were always pulling me out and bringing me home wet, but I don't remember that.

Once in a while I'd play with my brother George, but two and a half years makes a lot of difference. He had friends of his own age, and I had mine. As a result, we weren't particularly close. We fought, once in a while, but not more than most brothers.

There was a lot of family life, too. We had relatives and friends who would often come over evenings and holidays. At that time, not too many people had radios or phonographs, so when we got together we'd sing. Somebody might have a beat-up accordion and just barely know how to play it. We would sing along with this. I still like Slovak music although I don't know too many songs.

Sunday afternoons we might watch a soccer game or maybe go to the woods to a picnic area. We'd take some bacon and bread and sit around a fire. As you're cooking the bacon and it starts to drip, you put it over the bread until the bread is soaked. I did this in 1967 when I took my wife Jill and daughter Meg back there and they got a kick out of it.

I didn't have too many duties, other than cleaning out the barn and the pigpen and maybe feeding the chickens and geese. I got bit in the arm by a goose one day when I was trying to stuff corn down her throat. I don't know whether she was mad or hungry. My brother and I would hoe and dig out potatoes and I can remember going in the fields with my mother to pick up the hay. We'd take the horse and a great big wagon. My mother would tie the hay in bales and I'd either be on top of the wagon stacking the bales neatly so we could get more in, or would be throwing them up to my brother.

My mother says I wasn't the easiest youngster to handle, but I don't remember being particularly bad. I know that my father, who died at Eastertime in 1965, wasn't as stern a father as I am. I don't remember his ever hitting me, although I'm sure I deserved it and probably did get punished.

The earliest thing in my life that I clearly remember is the first day I went to school. It was a small school, six or seven classes all together in one room, with maybe forty children. I panicked after I was in there ten or fifteen minutes and ran out of the place up into the hills where the village cowherd was

The Gift of a Child / 17

taking care of the cows. My mother had nearly everybody in the village looking for me. They dragged me back to school.

I enjoyed school after that, and I still don't know why I ran away. Even now, certain things frighten me. There are times when I'm supposed to go somewhere and I really get shook up about it. I don't always know the reason. I get tense and nervous about it and have to force myself to go. I was like that as a child in Czechoslovakia, that first day in school. Running up to the hills was the first thing I thought of because there I was comfortable. I had a passion for the hills and helping the men, whether they were herding sheep or cows. I imagine it was a matter of mood. Not that I was a loner. I didn't consider myself a loner when I was alone and I didn't consider myself overly friendly when I was with the others. I just didn't necessarily need to be with someone to be content.

Maybe I learned to like school because I liked the teacher, Mr. Pagac—a short, balding man who wore glasses. He had a daughter, Tanya, who was a cute little thing and it could be I also liked school because I had a crush on her. But Mr. Pagac was very understanding, and I got the impression that all teachers were like him. I wasn't a remarkable pupil but I did well enough.

Of course, I was too young to know much about World War II, which ended when I was five years old. My only strong recollection of it is that two German soldiers were billeted with us —in that tiny apartment—for a while. They were nice to me and sent me to the canteen to get their food. Once in a while they would give me some candy. When they were on the rifle range, one of them held the gun and let me pull the trigger. Of course, I had no real idea of who they were or what they represented.

In the late spring of 1948, my uncle Joe Mikita and his wife Anna, who had emigrated to St. Catharines, Ontario, Canada, years before, came back for a visit of six months. Ten years before, when my brother George was born, Uncle Joe had sent my parents a congratulatory telegram. It ended, kiddingly or not, "When the next one is born I'm going to come over and get him."

My mother and father didn't think anything more about what he said. They thought he was joking and then the war came and by the time I was born they had forgotten all about it. But he sent another letter, saying, "Don't forget what I said.

I'll be coming over to get him," although it wasn't until 1948 that he and my aunt could come. They were still childless and, even if my folks didn't realize it at first, were serious about wanting to take me back with them. At first, when my uncle brought this up again, my mother kept putting him off as if he were joking. But finally she realized that he was dead serious. He kept pressing her and my father, explaining what life was like in Canada and the opportunities that were available. Finally, Mom and Dad consented.

I remember sitting up one night in bed, listening to them talk in the kitchen part of the house. I got hungry and went to the door and asked for a piece of bread with jam and a glass of milk. My mother said, "We're busy, go back to bed." So I climbed back in bed and I could still hear them talking about taking me back to Canada, my mother saying, "Well, I don't think he wants to go." I started to cry at this time because I wanted the bread, and she thought I was crying because she wouldn't let me go to Canada. When she heard me cry she said, "Okay, you can have him." I've always wondered about that, how a mix-up can so change a man's life. I cried because I wanted the bread with jam, and as it turned out it affected my whole life.

I wanted to go. I was an adventurous eight-year-old, looking forward to going on a big boat to a country my uncle had told me so much about. I hung around him all the time he was visiting to hear about Canada and the United States. He seemed so wealthy to me; I thought all Canadians and Americans were millionaires and I wanted to see what it was like there. I didn't think about not coming back. They told me I was going on a visit to Canada, just going for a while. Actually, I suppose if I hadn't liked it I could have gone back. I don't know. Nobody asked me.

The trip seemed like a great adventure. The train to Prague was the first one I ever rode and Prague was the first city I ever had been in. The buildings seemed so high to me—although, in comparison with cities here, they really weren't—that I walked down the street with my nose up in the air. Bumping into a light pole cured me of that.

My first shock came when we were in the station in Prague, ready to board the train that was to take us to Le Havre, France, where we were to take a ship for Montreal. When I saw that the train was ready to pull out and that my mother

The Gift of a Child / 19

and father were going to be left behind, I wrapped my arm around a pole and cried. Every inch of the train ride I plotted to jump off and go back to my mother and father. It didn't make any difference that I wasn't the only child the Mikitas were taking back to Canada. They had also persuaded my aunt's family to let them take a niece, Irene Gonda. She's three years older than I am, and I now call her my sister, although I also have a younger sister, Viera, born in 1950 in Czechoslovakia.

We took a ship named the *Carinthia* from Le Havre to Montreal and I was seasick only once, although the voyage took two weeks. One thing that sticks in my mind about the trip is Irene's coming up to me on board and offering me some gum.

"Here," she said, "this is from Dad."

"Dad? My Dad's back in Czechoslovakia."

"No," she went on, "this is from your new Dad."

"Are we going to call him Dad now?" I asked.

"I guess so," was her reply.

And we did. I just accepted it and I've called Uncle Joe and Aunt Anna Dad and Mom ever since. That's the way I think of them.

I remember arriving in St. Catharines for the first time three days before Christmas in 1948. It's a beautiful little city in southern Ontario not too many miles from Buffalo and that day the ground was covered with three feet of snow—more than I had ever seen before.

At the time my uncle lived at 57 Hamilton Street in a two-bedroom house to which he had added two bedrooms upstairs. It was a modest, clean home and I thought it was a palace. But the thing that really grabbed me was the kitchen, complete with a refrigerator that had a light that went on when the door opened. I think I played with it for hours when I discovered the light was out when the door closed.

Back home we had used kerosene lamps though electricity is fairly common now. So the things that impressed me most in my new Canadian home were the electrical appliances and the fact that we cooked in one part of the house and slept in another.

It didn't take long for me to meet the kids in the neighborhood or to learn about hockey, but it wasn't easy. When I tired of looking around the house, I began looking out of the window at the snow packed three or four inches deep on the streets. I saw the kids playing road hockey without skates and at first I just watched out of the window until my new mother suggested I go out and get some fresh air.

So I stood on the front porch and watched a while. The next thing I knew I was on the sidewalk not fully knowing what the boys were doing or how to say anything. I didn't understand a word of English but I noticed a few times the boys would look over at me and then talk among themselves. I knew they were talking about me.

Next day, from my sidewalk position I watched them again and this time they were short a player until a kid named Bob Johnson, who was three years older than me, handed me a stick. Grabbing my arm he pulled me out into the street and using a kind of sign language explained, "These guys are against those guys and you're against me!"

It's funny, but Bob handed me my first stick and he's the first player I hit.

The shinny game was barely under way when he came at me with the puck trying to go around. It seemed obvious the object was to stop him so I whacked him on the shins with my stick. When he stopped yelling Bob realized I didn't know any better and after shaking his head to explain that was against the rules, he grabbed my arms and slapped my hands on my stick. Then he started to show me how to stick-handle, sliding the puck and then shooting.

I guess that has to be the start of the whole thing; my hockey career really started right that second.

That was a long time ago and things have happened to me in hockey that I never would have dreamt of in those days. I realize that just having the chance to play didn't make me a hockey player, at least not one good enough to get into the National Hockey League and win some trophies along the way. I'm just average height and weight and, though I may have quicker reflexes than most men, a fellow needs something else if he's going to get an edge in professional sports. Maybe it's a question of trying a lot harder. Or always wanting to do better, never settling for second best, always trying to be first in anything—whether hockey, golf, ping-pong or polo.

I don't know if I was that way at the start; I was too young to know. Sure, I always wanted to do better than the last time. If I got "D" in school I wanted to get "C." If I got "C" I wanted to get "B." It wasn't that I was mad at anybody; I just

The Gift of a Child

wanted to be better for my own satisfaction. That's the way it was at first. But coming to Canada changed me. I think it made the feeling of wanting to excel more intense.

I was homesick to start with. When I was asked, "What do you want to be when you grow up?" I'd answer, "I want to join the air force and be a pilot so I can go home, go back to see my mother and father." I don't think that I ever resented my mother and father for having sent me away with my new parents, but I always had this thing in the back of my head that I wanted to go back.

Maybe it was a feeling that I didn't really belong in Canada or in any other place different from what I was used to. Feeling like an outsider is unpleasant, frustrating and confusing. Among the first words I heard from the Canadian boys were "foreigner" and "DP" and even before I knew what the words meant their tone stung me like a sharp knife. This is probably when I became so intense about winning, when I became a scrapper. It must have been my way of shouting to the world, "Maybe I am a foreigner but I'll prove I'm better than you are."

Even now I'm not satisfied, though probably I shouldn't feel that way any more because of the silverware I've won, the league scoring championships and the All-Star Team selections. Sure, I received those trophies and appreciate the honor, but it doesn't mean that much to me now, although it will when I'm through playing and look back. Right now I hardly think about it. Winning a hockey game, even an exhibition, is more important, and I always get a big kick out of it. It bothers me, I take it hard if we're losing. Heck, I'd even like to pick up the Vezina trophy and that's impossible, since it goes to goaltenders. But you know what I mean.

It isn't up to me to analyze these things. All I know is that I feel that having come to Canada from Czechoslovakia had something to do with making me the sort of person I am. If I only know one way of doing anything—to do my darndest and play to win—I think it grew out of a feeling I had to do better than anyone else.

3

A "DP" Tries Harder...
He Has To

IT MUST be a good sign that I can laugh about it now. It shows how far I've come since childhood, when taunts like "DP" (Displaced Person, then; Delayed Pioneer, my definition now) and "foreigner" infuriated me. Not that I've come to appreciate being taunted or hearing anyone being teased, but I've learned the absurdity of such thoughtless acts.

More than anything else, something that happened between me and Henri Richard of the Montreal Canadiens a few years ago made me aware of how ridiculous name-calling can be. Richard and I always have had a touchy relationship. We've even had a fight or two or more. I treasure one of those with him, because it's one of the few I've ever won. I can't fight my way out of a paper bag, and I can probably identify the ceilings in a lot of rinks I've played in.

What usually touched off our scraps was a stick or elbow in the right place. Henri would call me "DP" and I'd snap back with "Frog" or "Pea Soup"—because he's a French Canadian. Words led to fists and penalties.

We both wound up in the penalty box one game after a fight. Then I guess Henri glared at me and I looked at him, and I kind of snickered. He said: "Say, what you laugh at? You a DP. You come to dees country. You even don' speak so pretty good da Engleesh." That heavy, broken accent sounded as funny as hell under the circumstances. I just sat back and roared while Henri fumed.

That's sure not the way I thought about it when I was a kid. I was sensitive, easily hurt, quick to anger, and green. I wonder how a kid could have known so little about some things.

Even after I arrived in Canada, I thought my new Dad—

like all Canadians—was a millionaire. I never thought any of the people worked. You needed money? It was always there.

I found out the truth a few weeks after I got to St. Catharines. I was used to getting up early, and Dad would get up at six o'clock. One morning, we had breakfast together and then he started putting on his coat.

Curiosity made me ask, "Where are you going this early?"

"I'm going to work," he said.

Now, that really stunned me. A man living in Canada, and he's going to *work!*

"What do you have to work for?"

"So I can feed you," he answered simply. Stan Mikita began to learn that you don't get something for nothing.

Dad worked hard. He came to Canada from the old country maybe twenty years before he brought Irene and me over. He started out as a carpenter, and after a time got on his own, became a construction contractor. He built houses . . . good ones. Every time he built a house, he'd sell our old one, and we'd move into the new one. We moved about six times in the first seven or eight years. I was about fourteen or fifteen when he built an apartment building. He went into hock for that, but he figured he wasn't getting any younger, that he needed an investment. He still owns it, but he and Mom live next door, in a four-bedroom house. You just know he built that one, too, and that's where I lived with them just before I went to play with the Black Hawks, in 1959.

Dad and Mom are pretty easy-going people. They weren't terribly strict with me or Irene, although they had definite ideas of what was right and what was wrong and how we should behave. And Dad wasn't above giving me a good smack on the behind if he thought I deserved it. Which I did, maybe more often than he gave it to me.

I suppose I got along better with Dad than with Mom—which may be standard. Maybe it was because she didn't know exactly how to handle me. I talked back to her if I thought I was right but then I still do that a little bit, to anybody. It just happened more often with her, and she'd get impatient. If I didn't make my bed in the morning she'd say, "Just wait until you get on your own and you'll learn how to make your bed." I imagine every boy has heard that a million times.

Dad wasn't much on giving me lectures. He did give one,

though, just before sending me off to Edith Cavell School, where I was to start in the third grade.

"First of all, if you're going to get along don't make the same mistake I did," he said. "I didn't bother to learn the language. I stuck with people of my own background, Slovak people. It took me a long time to learn English, even to understand it. It'll be easier for you, but you're going to have to work at it, too. Every chance you get, try to learn as much as you can. I want you to do well in school, to work hard."

Dad knew a fellow carpenter, also a Slovak, who had a daughter going to the same school. Her name was Norma Lansky, and she was a little older. She took me in to see the principal and then to a Miss Patterson, who was to be my third-grade home-room teacher. Norma explained everything to me. She was my interpreter . . . and I sure needed one. I came to school knowing just one complete sentence of English. Luckily, I had asked Dad how I was going to tell the teacher I wanted to go to the washroom. Dad told me to say, "May I go to the bathroom, please?"

With that vocabulary, I didn't last more than two days in the third grade. I was promoted to kindergarten. Did I ever learn! In three weeks I improved my English to the point where I could be returned to the third grade with kids my own age.

That's the real way to learn and retain a language, in my opinion. Get in a situation among the natives where you sink or swim. Even today, I like to brush up on my Slovak by talking with a neighbor, from time to time.

Miss Patterson took me under her wing. Every time she asked a question of the whole class she'd say, "Stanley, do you understand what I'm talking about?" I didn't want to appear different from the other kids or out of place so I'd say, "Sure," although I often had no idea what she had asked. I didn't want the kids looking over their shoulder at me and saying, "Oh, here's a dummy." I didn't want to be different. Don't forget, to a child that age everything is magnified in importance and his feelings are extremely sensitive. At least, mine were. I was afraid they would be hurt if I was thought of as different, as a DP. I felt I had to be part of the group, that I couldn't appear to be inferior. It took a certain amount of acting and it really didn't work because the English language is so difficult and even if I could get the gist of a sentence there were so many words that sounded alike yet had different meanings, like their and there.

I really couldn't fool Miss Patterson or the other teachers, though. When they'd ask a specific question I'd give an answer that would have nothing at all to do with what they were talking about. Miss Patterson caught on quickly. She'd keep me after class and say, "Obviously you don't understand the question from the way your answer is worded." Then I would admit, "No, I don't." She would explain things thoroughly. I could have saved a lot of time and trouble if I had admitted in the first place that I didn't understand, but I felt it was beneath me to make a mistake or admit not understanding something everyone else did.

Miss Patterson taught mostly arithmetic, and maybe she judged me a little more kindly because I was good at it. If she gave us a problem in addition, I'd be adding up the numbers as she read them off and I'd usually be either the first or second kid to have the right answer. It got to be a contest. There's one thing that Miss Patterson told me that I'll never forget. She said, "Stanley, don't ever be afraid if you don't know something to ask what it is, why it is that way, how it got that way." I can't think of anyone giving me much better advice than that.

Years later, when I was with the Black Hawks and home in St. Catharines for a visit, I met Miss Patterson while walking on St. Paul Street. She was just as interested than as to how I was doing as she had been in me as a youngster. She was the first person in Canada outside of my family who took an interest in me and made an extra effort to teach me and I will be always grateful to her for that.

As I said, perhaps it was my aptitude for mathematics that made her take an extra interest in me. I think that skill in mathematics and a natural aptitude for knowing angles is helpful in hockey. As a boy I played a lot of billiards and I learned that, basically, you can play a puck the same way as you play a billiard ball if you use the angles. This has helped me in the bank shots on the ice and especially off the backboards.

The facility with math also hasn't hurt when it comes to negotiating a contract. That's one time I can hold my own when it comes to tossing figures around.

I wish I had been as interested in or as eager to do well in other subjects. Not that I had much trouble in school, at least, not until a lot later on in high school. But I didn't want to seem overly smart in grade school. If you were a "brain," kids looked down on you and called you "teacher's pet." If you were in the middle of the pack you were accepted, which was extra important to me. I wish now I had had the guts to try for the best grades all through school. I don't know if I was smart enough to head the class, but I should have tried. I did want to do better, but I let outside pressure steer me off. I hope my youngsters always do their best, regardless of their ability. There's something sad about it if you don't.

It didn't take me long to get together with some boys of my own age. We had our "gangs," although the word is in disfavor nowadays because it makes you think of black leather jackets and knives or guns. But this 1949 gang meant a bunch of guys hanging around together, playing baseball, lacrosse, hockey, soccer and football. I knew a lot of boys and made some good friends because I took part in all these sports.

We weren't just a bunch of roughnecks, but I seldom backed away from a battle. Maybe I should have overlooked the things some of the kids said about my accent or fractured English. But, often feeling like an outsider, like I didn't really belong, I had just two weapons . . . to outshine them in a game or try to punch them in the mouth.

Dad never interfered. I remember one time running into the house looking for sympathy after taking a pretty good beating, Dad didn't give me any.

"Listen, you'd better learn to stand up on your own two feet. You just can't come in crying every time somebody punches you in the nose. If you can't take care of yourself, don't get in a fight in the first place."

My best friend was Archie Maybe who lived across the street from school and was in my class. We started chumming together because we had the same interests, mostly sports. He was a good little skater, and we'd both hang around with the bigger kids. They knocked us around every time we got out of line, but they never really drove us away because they were always looking for an extra guy for whatever game they were playing. In a way, playing with the bigger kids was a help. I had to go all out in order to keep up with them and that stuck with me. Try harder and show you belong.

I never had a pet because my mother was against it. I didn't mind, though, because Ronnie Tempest, a kid across the street, had a dog and I thought of him as my own. Prince was mostly collie, black with white spots. He used to follow me part way to school in the morning and I'd have to shoo him away. After school, he'd be right back, running after me, licking my hands. That's how he got killed, running across the street after me. I didn't see him hit by the car, I just heard the thud, turned around and there he was, laid out in the street. I grabbed him in my arms and I still can remember the blood flowing all over me. I swore then I'd never have a dog because it was too big a heartbreak for me when Prince was killed. You can't build those kinds of protective walls, though, and now that I have children, we have a dog and I enjoy Heidi as much as they do.

Our family in St. Catharines was closely knit, and when I was small I went everywhere Dad and Mom did. They often took Irene and me to Toronto in the summer for what was called Czechoslovakian Days, picnics almost every Sunday. I spent most of the time kicking a soccer ball around and stuffing myself. Other Sundays we would go to the beach near St. Catharines. Then there were the Saturday nights at the Slovak Hall—but I soon broke away from that. What was a kid going to do there? I would rather be out skating or seeing a movie.

More and more, sports began to take over my entire life. I seldom read a book. If we had to read something from the library for school I did it, but never unless it was required. I wish now I had made the time to read. I've got one of those home-study reading improvement courses now, and hope to increase my reading speed and make up for that loss.

In the early fall of 1949 Dad took me to a public skating session, after buying me a pair of second-hand skates. They were too large for me, but Dad figured that I could grow into them and so use them for two or three years. I had to stuff the toes but I was able to skate on them without much trouble and they did last until 1952. Fortunately, they were hockey skates, not figure skates, although I really don't know that Dad at the time knew the difference.

I wouldn't recommend a parent's buying a pair of skates that are so large you have to stuff the toes or the foot slides around in the boot. I do feel that rather than buying cheap skates because a younger child's feet grow so fast, it's wiser to get a good pair with built-in protection and wear two heavier pairs of socks at first, going down to one thinner pair as the feet grow. If the skates are too large, there's a good chance of twisting an ankle. If they're too small, it's uncomfortable to skate in them for any length of time. I was either lucky or had strong ankles, so I was able to make do with that first pair of skates, and as soon as I got them I was doing a lot more skating than reading.

The most important thing I read at that time was an article in the newspaper about the Canadian Legion's starting a hockey league for boys between the ages of twelve and fourteen. Registration was to be on two successive Saturday mornings at the St. Catharines rink, and Archie and I decided to try to enroll, although we were a couple of years under the minimum age that fall of 1949.

The first Saturday at the rink, we tried to tell the man doing the registering that we were small for our age, but he sent us home. We were back the next Saturday, and made sure we saw someone else. He pretended to believe our story and let us enroll.

Dad knew that I was going to play organized hockey, but didn't say much about it. We never discussed hockey, baseball or football. But he did keep a close eye on the boys I was chumming with and would have said something if he didn't like something about them. He would always ask where I was going and when I got back he'd ask where I had been. He kept tabs on me, but on a loose string. He knew that I had enrolled in the hockey league.

We were to watch the newspaper to learn which team we would try out for. They could put only fifteen or twenty boys on a squad, which meant that with six teams only about one-third of all who had registered would eventually make the grade.

You can imagine how Archie and I waited for the newspaper each day, and how excited we were when our names appeared, although we were on different teams. He was on the Montreal club, and I was on the New York Rangers. But we didn't mind that so much because we were still playing together at school.

I showed up at the rink with my second-hand skates and gloves and a stick. The boots were too big, but I had stuffed the toes with paper and I had magazines tied around my shins for protection. It wasn't until several years later that I got a pair of good skates. Dad paid $23 for them, which was a lot of

A "DP" Tries Harder ... He Has To / 29

money in 1952. By that time I was playing so much hockey and doing well enough that I needed a better pair of skates and Dad wanted his son to be equipped as well as anybody else. This first day, though, I must have been a sight. Anyway, we skated a little, then went right into scrimmage. Being younger than most of the kids, I just dug and dug—harder than ever before. I must have impressed Bill Buschlin and Dennis White, who were coaching the Rangers, enough to keep me. They told me to get some regular shin pads and pants.

Dad didn't know much about hockey, and it took a little pleading to get him to buy me the equipment. Finally, he gave in, but he never did pay much attention to hockey until I was older. I really think it was a good thing.

Buschlin and White had played Junior-A hockey for St. Catharines, and later a little Senior-A. Both knew the game well, but by this time they had jobs outside of hockey and coaching was just something they did because they loved the game and enjoyed teaching youngsters how to play. Men of this kind are the backbone of the game.

I think organized sports are terrific for the sake of any kids. If my son Scott wanted to get in the Peewee program in hockey, I'd be pleased but I would stay out of the picture. I'd leave it up to his coaches. I would never interfere in a game or a practice, whether the coach was right or wrong. These fellows put in a lot of their leisure time coaching, and they deserve respect and a free hand. A parent should be grateful enough in knowing that by helping his boy participate in sports the coach is keeping him off the streets and out of trouble.

Parents also can contribute to making the hockey program successful and in making the coach's job easier. They can do it both by supporting their local hockey programs with their own money and by helping to raise funds. Ice time is costly and rink charges, like everything else, are steadily rising. Parents can volunteer to drive youngsters to rinks and games. A parent can make sure that a child has the proper protective equipment. This makes the coach's job easier and relieves his mind, as he doesn't have to worry about sending a boy on the ice with the chance that he might be injured because he is not thoroughly protected.

Maybe that's what Dad thought. Anyway, he and Mom didn't come to a game until I was twelve or thirteen and was playing bantam hockey. I remember that because I got rapped hard against the boards, just below where they were sitting, and fell down. Mom was sitting only five or six rows away and I heard her scream in broken English, "Oh, Stanley, are you hurt?"

I was so embarrassed, I was hoping the ice would melt and swallow me up. I mumbled, "No, I'm all right," wishing she and Dad hadn't come.

To make things worse, when I got home Mom said, "That's it—that's the last game you are ever going to play. No more hockey. It's too rough."

I had to beg to make her change her mind and let me play again.

All that came later. The first day of organized hockey with the "New York Rangers" I was on my own—and on the bench most of the time with the rest of the little guys. "Montreal" did it again . . . we lost 10-1. I remember that Frannie Stewart, who later became a pal, did pretty well with nine goals and an assist. His own teammates worked hard trying to swipe a chance with the puck.

I wasn't a bench-warmer too long. The following year and the year after that it seemed as if I played almost sixty minutes a game. I had gotten my start in organized hockey, and couldn't get enough of it.

4

The Rink Rats

I SHOULD have been impressed the first time I met Doug Harvey, Maurice (Rocket) Richard, Bernie (Boom Boom) Geoffrion and two or three other players of the Montreal Canadiens. I wasn't. I had no idea how famous they were, or what they represented.

Often now I read about some young player coming into the league saying his boyhood idol was Gordie Howe, Rocket Richard or Jean Beliveau, and that's why he took up hockey or developed a certain style. I can't say that. I had no hero. It even took me a long time to realize that money could be made playing hockey, and I know that until I was eighteen I didn't think about making my living at it.

Anyway, I first met some of the Canadiens just before I turned thirteen. I was going to Victoria School then and the school principal was Ashton Morrison, who had been president of the Ontario Minor Hockey Association and had known Frank Selke Sr., manager of the Canadiens, the Stanley Cup champions of 1952-53. The Canadiens were stopping over at St. Catharines and Morrison invited Selke to bring some of the players to Victoria School. I asked for autographs just because the other kids were doing it.

Morrison later told me that just in fun Selke had asked, "Would you like to make a deal for one of our players?" Morrison had replied, "No, I wouldn't trade Mikita for any of them." When Morrison told me about the incident at the time, I figured he was trying to make me feel good, but I think he sincerely meant it.

Morrison was high on me because I had a hand in helping Victoria win the city public school hockey championship in 1953. The next year my folks moved again, and I attended Prince of Wales School. As it turned out, Morrison also had moved, becoming principal of Prince of Wales. We won the city championship there in 1954.

Jim Patterson, a young fellow right out of college, was in charge of sports at Prince of Wales and coached the hockey team. He taught me about sportsmanship, stressing fair play, trying not to play dirty, and not being a sore loser. That last never quite hit home with me. I'm a bad loser and I admit it though it doesn't tear me to pieces for more than a couple of hours after a game. When I cool off enough to realize we lost because the opposing team was better than we were, I shrug off the defeat and resolve to do better next time. But right after a losing game I'm not easy to talk to.

Most of my hockey I learned first from Buschlin and White, who ran the Legion teams, and then Vic Teal, coach of the bantam team and chief engineer at the St. Catharines Arena. The Legion teams were more than just an excuse for kids to have a shinny game; it was organized play. We went up and down our wings, for example, instead of just chasing the puck all over the place. Some fine players came off those teams. Gerry Cheevers, Elmer (Moose) Vasko, Ray Cullen and Doug Robinson, among others, later made it to the National Hockey League.

There's no comparison between playing shinny and belonging to an organized team with good coaches in charge. It stands to reason that if somebody is coaching you he's going to spot your mistakes and correct them right on the spot, so you'll learn to play the game the right way. If you play shinny, most of the kids have only one thought in mind, to score as many goals as they can, without worrying one bit about backchecking and all the other fundamentals of the game. Playing on a regular team is almost essential if you want to advance in hockey and your ultimate goal is to play in the NHL.

I was fortunate to have expert coaching and regular play from the start. And I was fortunate in another respect. I could advance all the way through the hockey program to the Junior-A level without leaving home, as did Vasko. Bobby Hull and many others weren't that lucky, and I say that because it must be a considerable strain on a boy of thirteen or fourteen when he is shipped from town to town as Bobby was. A boy at this age is liable to get homesick, sometimes finds it difficult to make friends right away, and is also likely to find too much

The Rink Rats

time on his hands. A boy who stays home can have guidance from his folks when he needs it, and doesn't have too much loose time because his friendships are formed and he knows pretty well what he's going to do most of the time.

In a way, a boy who leaves home does have a few advantages, from the hockey standpoint. Not as much is expected of him in a strange town as is at home, where people are more familiar with how well he can play. There were moments when I was hoping I could leave home, but I think I was lucky, as it turned out, to do all my playing in St. Catharines.

When I was thirteen it seemed as if hockey was my whole life. I was playing on three teams, "The Rangers," the school, and the City Bantam, which was like an all-star squad from the Legion League. I was playing four games a week and when I wasn't in a game I was hanging around the rink. I had become a "Rink Rat."

Rink Rats had been in existence long before I came. It was like a club. We even had a little room in the rink, with three or four cots in it so we could sleep there. We dusted seats, swept the arena after games, scraped and flooded the ice, and did odd jobs. In exchange we got free ice time. We showed up at the rink at 6 A.M., when Teal got there, and practiced a couple of hours before school. After school we'd practice another hour, get in on two hours of public skating, and maybe have a little game going until midnight.

Dad didn't mind my spending so much time at the rink because at that time school came easy for me and I was getting along all right. I guess he figured that as long as I was at the rink I couldn't get into too much trouble.

Dad could be sure of one thing: I was in good hands with Teal, a solidly built guy who had been a minor-league hockey player and was about forty-five at this time. Teal had been chief engineer at the rink since 1938 and started coaching kids' teams the next year. He was a tough son of a gun, but had a heart of gold. If you were ever stuck for anything, he'd slip you a couple of dollars. After a game, he'd buy the refreshments for the team out of his own pocket. His wife (Ma Teal, we called her) was just as good-hearted as he was. She would make us a stack of sandwiches, even if we were just going on a short road trip. But he was tough. He gave an outward impression that if you looked at him the wrong way you'd be sorry. As is often the case with people, it was a hard shell. I owe more to Teal than to anyone else in hockey. He taught me the fundamentals I needed to become a good hockey player.

When I came to him I had bad playing habits. I didn't know how to body-check properly, and if I was beaten on a play I tended to lose my head. I might give my opponent the butt end of the stick or slash him or swing with my fists. Teal taught me how to check and play a man. He showed me how to keep an opponent between me and the boards so he couldn't get by on the inside toward center ice. That way, even if he did have a step or two on me, he couldn't cut in and I could always steer him out.

Teal stressed defense and fundamentals; the shooting, he said, could come later. He forced us to be two-way skaters. What I mean is that most youngsters skate counterclockwise, the right foot crossing over, which is the natural way. Every practice, Teal would make us skate the other way, clockwise, the left foot crossing over.

He used gimmicks to improve our game. He hung cans in the nets for us to shoot at and placed barrels on the ice to stickhandle around; he laid wooden planks on the ice surface to flip the puck over to improve passing. I learned to pass off my backhand as well as my forehand. He kept us at these drills endlessly, and they paid off.

At the time I didn't appreciate what he was doing for me and I guess I was sassy. He didn't like that and he'd give me a whack on the behind with a broom for talking back or not following instructions. He would boil over if he caught us smoking. Once in a while, like most kids will, we would sneak a cigarette, and Teal's stormy reaction to that would have made a great TV commercial about why you shouldn't smoke.

The biggest blowup of all wasn't my fault. At least, I didn't start it. We had a big, burly defenseman who didn't get along at all with Teal, didn't like the way he would tell us what to do. If you didn't pass the puck right, Teal would come up with the broom and whack you one on the seat. The defenseman figured he was too big to be treated that way and started swearing at Teal and told him to "go jump in the lake." I had to chime in, "Yeah, go jump in the lake," adding a word or two that wasn't quite as innocent.

Teal blew up: "Get out of here! I never want to see you two kids here again."

"You can't kick us out of here," I shot back. "This is a public place. We work here."

"Not any more you don't," Teal said, grabbing his favorite broom. "I'll show you if you can stay here or not." And he swept us out of the rink. Then he passed the word to all the employees in the building to make sure Mikita and his pal didn't get back in.

I stayed away two days. At first I thought this would be a good time to catch up on my schoolwork, but that didn't take long. Then I didn't know what to do with myself. The rink was my whole life at the time and I had lost it. I decided to go back and apologize.

At first, Teal wouldn't even see me. "I don't want to talk to you," he said.

I wouldn't leave. "I want to apologize for the way I talked to you. I'm sorry about the whole thing. I really mean it," I told him.

He wasn't convinced. "I don't think you do," he said. I started crying, and I guess that showed him how sincere I was and how much it meant to me.

"All right, you can come back," he said. "But make sure I don't catch you swearing, smoking, or anything like that."

I did quit smoking. If I sneaked one cigarette a day at that time, it was because it was the thing to do, the other boys did it. I didn't smoke again until I was eighteen and I'm not a heavy smoker now, though it would have been better to avoid the habit altogether.

I was with Teal three seasons, first on the Bantam team, then on the Midget, so he got to know me pretty well. We keep in touch now, and before I started writing this book I asked him to describe his recollections of me at the time. He was kind enough to jot down some comments, and the phrase that caught my attention was this: "but [Mikita] had something inside him to be the best. He was always trying to prove he was as good as the others."

Teal was perceptive and saw a little of what was going on inside my head as I tried to prove I was as good as other people. I just didn't believe it. If I had, I could have avoided some trouble and also some lesser annoyances.

For instance, I might have managed more dates with girls sooner than I did. I was such a roughneck a few girls turned me down and one incident about Ginny Dillon—who ended up marrying a good friend of mine—stands out in my memory. I wanted to take her out but was too shy to bring it up, though I finally got up enough nerve to ask her to go to a party with me. My dad had a 1952 half-ton pickup truck which he used in his business, and I couldn't see how I could drive a girl anywhere in this. How would she feel getting all dressed up and going on a date in a pickup truck? Finally, Ginny said fine, and I took her to the party in the truck and we had an enjoyable evening. I know I did, and I think she did, too. It's funny how a kid's mind works at that age. It was a nice truck and I had spent four hours washing it, making sure the seats were clean, but I thought she would be embarrassed going in a truck, yet it didn't faze her a bit.

I have to admit that after I started dating I wasn't the biggest spender in the world. None of us had much money, so if we'd go to a movie we'd meet the girls inside. We might spring for soft drinks and ice cream after the show.

The first time I really made any money was one summer when Teal got me a job working at Municipal Beach on Lake Ontario at Port Weller. There were four or five of us, and we kept the beach clean, picking up papers and scrap. If it was busy, I'd direct traffic onto the parking lot. We even slept there, on cots in the concession building. It was a nice way to spend two months and I met some interesting girls.

But at that time girls were a spare-time occupation; my mind was mostly on sports. I played soccer through the eighth grade, when we won the city championship at Prince of Wales School. I played lacrosse on the city team and I remember Gerry Cheevers, who later became goalie for the Boston Bruins, was a tremendous lacrosse player. I think lacrosse is even better as far as conditioning goes than hockey; you're always moving, you can't glide. I also played basketball my first two years in high school but I wasn't that good at it. I could pass, but I couldn't put the ball in the basket.

Next to hockey, my best sport might have been baseball. The Canadian Legion also had a baseball league and I joined that, too. I became a catcher because I didn't have any money to buy a glove to play the other positions and the team supplied the catcher's equipment. I liked to hit and had pretty fair power, but if I had a choice I would rather be behind the plate than at bat. It was more of a challenge because you control the pitcher. There's more teamwork—two guys working together. At bat, you're strictly on your own.

I played baseball on a provincial-league team until my last year of junior hockey, when I was eighteen; then I had my shoulder broken playing hockey and couldn't throw anymore. At the time, two major-league scouts were interested in me. I was told the Chicago White Sox and Philadelphia Phillies were thinking about inviting me to camp for a tryout. That was in 1958, and I probably would have gone just to see what it was like. I don't know if it would have gone beyond that. But this was a "fast" league and several pretty good players, who later went on into professional baseball, came out of it.

Then there was football. First I played on the junior team, which was for the younger boys at high school. I was an end until I switched to the senior team, when I became a halfback. The other halfback was Bobby Hull, who in 1955 had come from Woodstock to play with the St. Catharines TeePees, the Junior-A hockey team.

Bobby was the power runner who went through the line. If some outside yardage was needed, they'd hand me the ball. I ran some pass patterns, too, because I always could catch the ball. We won the senior provincial championship one year, and I scored a few touchdowns.

Strangely, as in baseball, I liked defense better than I did offense. One of the things I remember best about playing football was a game in which I played safety on defense. A runner on the other team had broken through the line, and I was the last obstacle between him and a touchdown. As he was dashing toward the sidelines I moved to cut him off. I don't know what made me do it, but instead of trying to tackle him—the smart move—I just reached for the ball, found it in my hands, and ran the other way seventy yards for a touchdown.

Hockey, though, was the big sport at St. Catharines, and if you were any kind of player it was your ambition to try and make it in that game. Anyway, I never thought of becoming a professional in any sport until the Chicago Black Hawks asked me, and even then I wasn't sure I wanted to be one. I knew I had been drafted by the Black Hawks organization when I was twelve or thirteen and that they had the pro rights on me. But it didn't mean very much. Nobody asked Dad to sign anything; he wasn't even approached.

I just belonged to them, that's all.

It couldn't happen today the way it did then, just picking up the paper at the age of twelve or thirteen and reading that the Chicago Black Hawks had the rights to my services if I ever became a professional. Now hockey has a universal draft of boys when they reach the age of twenty. You can play for the TeePees and still be in the common pool of players to be drafted when eligible. It has been said that this isn't good from a humane standpoint, but I don't know how else hockey can assure a fair distribution of players. All other sports have similar systems, although I'd have to say that no longer is it likely, even in hockey, that a boy of thirteen could be drafted.

With all these sports the year around, you would think there wouldn't be enough time for me to get in trouble. I wish it had been like that, but in looking for approval and wanting to belong, I fell in with a rough bunch—despite the decent friends I had.

St. Catharines, like most cities, had its tough street gangs. And this time I *am* talking about the black-leather-jacket variety. I hung out with the Facer Street Gang, named after the district in which we lived. There were a lot of different ethnic groups in this area—Polish, Italian, Slovak, and others. The kids in the gang were rough and tough. Most of them were older than I was, and they didn't include me on all their escapades. They did a lot of petty thievery, and some that wasn't so petty—like stealing cars. I never got in trouble, but the cops would stop me sometimes and tell me to stay away from that group. But I admired the gang members because they were so "tough," I liked their company and they seemed not to mind having me around. It was easier to be accepted and feel a sense of belonging.

I was sixteen and had finished playing Midget hockey by this time. In the fall of 1956, the Junior TeePees opened training camp, and I wondered why I hadn't been invited. (The program was for kids from out of town, but I didn't know it.) Donnie Carr, a hockey buddy who hung around with another gang, and I went to Rudy Pilous, then TeePees coach, and asked, "Are you going to give us a tryout or not?" He looked at us and I could see what he was thinking. We both had greasy hair, long and dirty, with a duck tail. Our style of clothes matched our hair.

The Rink Rats / 39

Finally he said, "Well, Mikita, you get your hair cut and wash behind the ears and I'll give you a tryout."

That was the moment I broke away from the gang, and I'm firmly convinced it was the instant at which I was saved from going to jail sooner or later. You may think I'm exaggerating, but a number of those guys did wind up in jail. I feel I'm lucky. And so, as it turned out, was Carr. He went to Hamilton and played hockey there a while.

I've never discussed with Dad why he didn't step in at some point and try to straighten me out. Maybe he understood me pretty well, and how teenagers react, and felt I'd fall in deeper if he forced me to stay away. I guess he also knew I would work something out if I ever came to the crossroads. He was right.

Looking back, I was mature in some respects, immature in others. I don't think it matters how old you are, you still have a little kid stuff in you. Fortunately, I was able to see that hockey meant more to me than trying to prove that I was "as good as" the guys in the Facer Street Gang.

5

The Link Is Formed

THERE WAS nothing so important as hockey in the sports pages of the *St. Catharines Standard,* our local newspaper. Every fall, before the season opened, it would give a large spread to the new members coming into town to play for the TeePees, the Junior-A team, which was just one step away from the big time. I remember one such spread in particular— with good reason. It was all about Bobby Hull, a boy who was going to play for the TeePees after having been a sensation on the Junior-B team at Woodstock the previous season.

This was 1955 and I was on the Midget team, a year away from the TeePees. But I remember wondering what kind of a guy Bobby was as far as hockey was concerned. Was he really as great as the story in the newspaper said? Would this mean that I couldn't get a spot on the team next year? Of course, I wondered that about every new player who got such a big spread, like John McKenzie (now with Boston in the NHL) when he came to the TeePees the following year, after he had set a junior league afire out West. The difference was— although I could have no idea at the time—that Bobby Hull's name and mine were to be connected in countless newspaper and magazine stories in the years to come. The link had been formed.

I first met Bobby through one of the boys on the football team, although I didn't play hockey with him until the next year, 1956, which was his last year on the TeePees and my first. At that time, we didn't pal around much together since he was a year and a half older and had his buddies while I had mine. But in so many ways he was the same type of guy then that he is now. He was just as nice to people, just as outgoing, as friendly to little old ladies—even to little young ladies.

What amazed me was the way Bobby played football and hockey. As I mentioned earlier, we were the halfbacks at St.

The Link Is Formed

Catharines Collegiate. Bobby was almost as big as he is now, with much the same physique although not as heavy. Our football styles, like our hockey styles, were different. I ran end plays, and if I carried the ball, I'd take the easy way and follow the blocking. Not Bobby. He was our power runner, and when he carried the ball and the blocking went to the right, he'd run to the left as if to say, "I'll run through these guys myself." That's the way it looked, and 99% of the time he'd do just that. I don't know what Jim McNulty, our coach (he later became a Member of Parliament), thought of the way Bobby played, but anyway Canadian high school football players don't stick as close to the book as do Americans.

Bobby was a helluva skater and he sort of played hockey like he played football. Instead of going around an opponent he'd smash in and go over the top of him. He still does, so he hasn't changed. Hull's shot is terrific, either the wrist or the slap shot, and that was the thing that impressed me most, plus the fact that he was such a strong skater.

I played only briefly on a line with him at St. Catharines. Rudy Pilous had just switched Bobby from center to left wing and had put me at right wing. We didn't play together long, although I continued on a regular line. But it was a third line and there were experienced players on the team who got more ice time than I did. I got eighteen goals and thought I had a pretty good season. Bobby had an even better season, for next fall, in 1957, he went to the Chicago Black Hawks to stay.

Rudy Pilous was still coaching the TeePees at the beginning of the 1957–58 season, though in January he took over the coach's job with the Black Hawks. Before he left, he made a decision that was to have a dramatic effect on my career—he switched me from right wing to center. I normally played right wing in the past since I favored that position—originally thinking that a right-hand shot played right wing, a left-hand shot left wing and, I guess, that a center was like a switch hitter in baseball, passing and shooting from either side. Of course, by the time Pilous called me in and suggested I become a center I knew better.

"You know, centers make a little more money than right wings," said Pilous. "You handle the puck well both forehand and backhand, you can pass both ways, you can skate, and you can stick-handle. This is what I need, a guy at center to do that kind of job. Also, you've got to look ahead a little. Look at that Chicago Club. They're pretty well stocked with right wingers. But who do they have to play center ice? Tod Sloan is getting on in age. Glen Skov isn't getting any younger. If you're going to make it anywhere, center ice is the spot."

All I said was, "Fine." If Pilous wanted me at center, that was all right with me, and as he said, I could handle the puck fairly well, forehand and backhand. It went back to what Vic Teal had taught us in fundamental drills, and now it paid off. But as for the reasons he gave as to why I should switch to center, that I'd have a better chance as a pro, I don't know how much weight that had with me. I was seventeen, but I still didn't realize guys were getting pretty good money to play hockey and nobody told me otherwise.

To give you an idea of what I knew about money:

When I first worked out with the TeePees in 1956, Pilous called me into his office just before the season started. "I think you could make this club, kid," he said. "I'll give you $25 a week. If you're still with the club after Christmas, I'll give you $35 a week."

Overwhelmed, I blurted out, "That's great, coach!"

As it turned out, I did well and he raised my pay to $35 after Christmas.

So the next year, before I went in to see him, I thought a long while about how I would get a pay hike from $35 to $50, which seemed like big money to me. I went in and said, "Rudy, I had a pretty good year and I think I ought to get $50."

He said, "I don't know, Stan. I don't think we can pay you that much. I know you had a fair year and you deserve a raise. I'll tell you what, I'll give you $40."

He acted like he was doing me a big favor, but I wasn't going to be easy game, so I said, "No, Rudy, I'm not going to start dangling one way or the other. If you want me to come down to $45, I won't. I'm going to stay at $50. If you don't give me $50, I'm not playing." I thought I was being smart and he went along with the gag.

He frowned, shrugged his shoulders and said, "Well, okay," as if he were being strong-armed, but he must have been laughing to himself because he got me so cheap.

That second year with the TeePees, I had a very good season. I got thirty-one goals, and I thought all summer about how I really was going to hold up Pilous this time. I knew the

The Link Is Formed / 43

limit for a Junior was $60 a week, but I had heard about players getting paid under the table. I just didn't know how to go about it, but I wasn't going to show Rudy I was ignorant. So I went in and started out, "Rudy, I want $60 a week."

He nodded, "Sure, Stan. That's all you can get anyway."

I said, "Yeah, I know, but I want $15 a week room and board." I was still living at home, but I wanted the $15 room and board for my mother.

Pilous shook his head: "I don't know if we can do it. I've got to balance the books and what am I going to say if they see an extra $15 on your check?"

I said, "Can't you give it to me in cash?" He finally agreed. I thought I had taken advantage of him, but I was just kidding myself because I heard later about a player who was making a National Hockey League salary while playing as a Junior. He got $7,500. And I was proud of myself for getting $3,900!

I played under Pilous only a year and a half at St. Catharines, Glenn Sonmor finishing the 1957–58 season after Rudy went to Chicago. Harry Watson coached the TeePees the next season. Each man had his own way of coaching, but naturally I got to know Pilous the best as I later played four years for him at Chicago.

Pilous had a tremendous gift of gab. He could talk more than anybody else I've ever known and was a great storyteller. I thought he was a good coach because he knew what he was talking about. Although, by the time a kid is playing Junior, you really can't show him that much since he should know the fundamentals. A coach at that level can work out different plays or spot flaws in a boy's skating or shooting. Or he can tell if a boy's not deking correctly, if he's using the same deke all the time. Pilous was good at correcting these mistakes and he could fire up a Junior team. In Junior hockey there's a lot of college rah-rah, something that doesn't go over with the older pros.

Pilous was a terrific orator before games and between periods. Sort of the Knute Rockne type, the kind of coach who says, with tears in his eyes, waving a postcard, "Here's a note from Johnny Doe, who's in the hospital with broken legs and arms and has mononucleosis. Let's win one for our old buddy, Johnny." Like every coach who ever lived, he had some favorite sayings. After a poor first period, he'd remark, "Geez, you guys couldn't beat the Nardiella girls from Buffalo." Or if you missed the net by a couple of feet on a slap shot: "Geez, you missed the net by as much as a farm boy could throw a big red apple."

Whenever he criticized or praised you, it would be privately, in his office. That is, unless you had made a couple of bad mistakes in a row, in which case he would fry your ears right in front of everybody. As for praise, it didn't matter to him how many goals or points you had scored, but only whether you had played well or not by his standards. If you had, he'd come up and say in a quiet way, "Son, you played a helluva game."

I learned more about Pilous later, when I joined him with the Black Hawks. He was a nervous individual in some ways, but I didn't really spot this as a Junior.

Sonmor coached us for just half a season, and then Watson took over my last year at St. Catharines. He didn't really tell us how to play individual games and we played them by ear. If it was a close-checking game, we played it that way; or if it was a wide-open game, that's the way we played it. Watson didn't try to set any particular pattern, maybe because he had a well-balanced club, a lot of good skaters and scorers and a sound defense. We had Matt Ravlich, Pat Stapleton, and Wayne Hillman playing defense, and guys like Johnny McKenzie, Chico Maki, Vic Hadfield, Denis DeJordy and others who later made the NHL. We won the league title that year by twenty points.

Most important, before the 1958-59 season ended I was thinking about turning pro. There were a couple of reasons. Stories were appearing in the newspapers, whether true or not, calling me "the best Junior hockey player in Canada." We played in Toronto, Montreal and Ottawa, and writers in those cities were kind to me. I started to think that if they're writing this kind of stuff, there must be something to it. And there was another reason for thinking of trying the pro life.

It started one evening in November, 1958, as I was at home eating dinner. The phone rang. It was Harry Watson.

"Listen, you'd better pack your bags," he said. "You've got a 12:15 (A.M.) train to catch out of Welland to go to Chicago. You're going to play there tomorrow night."

I sort of laughed, I didn't believe him. "Come on, Harry, you're pulling my leg," I said.

The Link Is Formed / 45

"I'm not kidding," he said. "I'll come on down at ten o'clock and drive you to the train."

Before I hung up the phone I said, "I won't pack my bag until you get here." I just couldn't believe him. I had heard of maybe one or two cases of Juniors going right up to the big league for a tryout, but I couldn't believe it would ever happen to me.

Usually a player spent a year or so, if not more, in the professional minor leagues before advancing to the NHL. Elmer Vasko played a few games in Buffalo before going to Chicago. Pat Stapleton and Matt Ravlich spent several years in the minors. Of course, now it's not uncommon for players to jump from Junior-A to the big league. Bob Pulford, Frank Mahovlich, Bobby Hull, Carl Brewer, and Dave Keon all went up just as I did without playing minor league hockey. But it wasn't common in 1958. At that time an amateur was allowed five games with a professional team without having to turn pro. He was paid $100 a game, so going to Chicago would be profitable as well as interesting, but I couldn't believe it.

Watson convinced me. He showed up early, helped me pack after explaining that Tod Sloan on the Chicago team had been hurt. Then he drove me the twenty miles to Welland where I was to have a sleeper on the train to Chicago. As luck would have it, the sleeper had been sold and I had to sit up all night. When I arrived I was limp with exhaustion, and I was to play that night.

Pilous was supposed to meet me at the LaSalle Street train station, but he was late and since I had no idea where the rink was I waited at the coffee counter. I was smoking a little at the time, and I thought I'd sneak a few puffs before Pilous showed up, even knowing that he didn't like his young players to smoke. I lit a cigarette, and no sooner was it in my mouth than there was a tap on my shoulder.

"Get rid of that damned cigarette," Pilous growled.

"Yessir," and right away I stomped it out. He took me to the Chicago Stadium, introduced me to trainer Nick Garen, and got me a uniform.

Pilous didn't give me a pep talk. He just said: "Try and do what you were doing at St. Catharines. Play the way you know how, that's all I expect of you."

Then he suggested, since I was going to be with the Hawks only a few days, that I stay with Bobby Hull, who was sharing an apartment in a western suburb with Ron Murphy and Tod Sloan. He had Garen put me on a Madison Street bus going west so I'd meet Bobby at the end of the line.

"Welcome to the club," Bobby said. "I know you're probably here just as a replacement right now, but you'll be up again next year."

I wasn't so sure.

My first game was against Montreal and it was only the second NHL game I had ever seen. The year before, the TeePees had an afternoon game in Toronto and they gave us standing room tickets to see the night game between the Maple Leafs and Hawks.

Pilous put me on the ice in a hurry, centering for left wing Ted Lindsay and right wing Ed Litzenberger. He couldn't have given me better support than two such outstanding veterans, and he couldn't have put me up against a tougher foe. My first job was to face off with "Big Jean" Beliveau, who is a fine gentleman on and off the ice but doesn't like to lose. There he stood, all six feet three of him, like a mountain, and I was shaking in my boots.

I thought, "Try your best. It's all that's expected of you." I had been good at taking face-offs and said to myself, "If you ever win one in your life, win this one." I'll be a son of a gun if I didn't get it back to the point and we got off a shot on the net. Right after that, I got off a shot of my own and also took a pretty good "check."

On the same shift, the puck came down into our end and the defenseman passed it out to me. All of a sudden, here I was coming down one-on-one against Doug Harvey, as good a defenseman as ever lived. I got cute, faked him to the right, and put the puck through his legs right on Jacques Plante, the goalie. Plante kicked the puck aside, but feeling pretty proud of myself I turned around to see where Harvey was and I didn't see Tom Johnson, the other defenseman, coming at me. He caught me with my head down and sent me flying through the air. I was shaken and it hurt, but I wasn't going to let on that it did, so I jumped right up and continued with the play.

I played three games with the Hawks before going back to St. Catharines. I didn't get a goal, but did get an assist on one by Lindsay for my first NHL point. I also got a taste for turning pro and started thinking that maybe I would try it for three or four years and see how it went.

The Link Is Formed / 47

I wasn't sure yet about turning pro the next fall. I was still eligible to play another year of Junior-A hockey and then the following year could go to camp again with the Black Hawks and listen to their offers. If they didn't meet my price, I could go back to school, finish high school, then go to college. I had several college athletic scholarship offers so the money would be no problem, and even then Dad had been saving money to send me to college. So there were still several choices ahead of me and I didn't feel any pressure to turn pro.

But I did start to think seriously about becoming a pro at this time. Not that I was sure of how good a player I was. I don't know even now how good a player I was, am, or ever will be. Even now when somebody compares me with other centers, say Beliveau, it doesn't mean anything to me. I know how well he plays because I've watched him in action. I've never seen motion pictures of myself play-by-play throughout a game so I really don't know what I can do on the ice. If I could watch every move through a game I would know better. Sure, I've seen television tapes of games I've played in, but the camera moves after the puck and you can't watch every move you make. So even now I'm not sure just how good I am, and you can imagine that it was that much more difficult for me to judge myself when I was nineteen. Still, playing with the Hawks briefly did give me a lift.

I don't know if that had anything to do with the way I played with the TeePees after I went back. I did win the scoring championship with 97 points on 38 goals and 59 assists, although I got into only 45 games. I missed some games because I suffered a broken wrist in the Junior-A All-Star game in January and continued playing, but I was through for the season when I dislocated my right shoulder February 12, 1959, and was operated on two days later.

I was chasing a puck, trying to get it before icing was called and as I turned a corner, trying to go behind the net, I slipped on a coin lying on the ice and started sliding head first into the boards. I caught myself with a little turn, and my right shoulder and head hit the boards. I could feel something snap and I knew right away it was serious. But I sat on the bench awhile until I found I couldn't lift my arm. When I was taken to the hospital my playing days were over at St. Catharines.

By this time Dad and Mom had gotten used to the idea of hockey players—like most athletes—suffering some injuries.

Three years before, when I was in Midget, we were in the provincial playoffs against the Toronto Marlies. Carl Brewer, who later played for the Maple Leafs, was on defense for them and had a habit of flipping the puck out of their end on his backhand. He was doing that as I came in on him and he caught me with his stick. It ripped my nose and cheek open, just missed the eye, cut the eyelid and eyebrow, going clear up to my forehead. I was rushed to the hospital and spent more than two hours as twenty-eight stitches were put in my face.

It had been a Saturday afternoon game, and I got back home in the evening. Mom and Dad were out so I let myself into the house, and went right to bed, with an awful headache. The whole right side of my face was bandaged and covered with an ice pack. I heard my parents come home but I just lay there.

Mom came into the room, flipped the light on, took one look at me and darn near passed out, screaming, "My God, what happened to you? I knew we shouldn't let you play hockey. You could have lost an eye, gone blind just to play a game. That's it, no more sports for you. You can forget about it. I don't want you killed."

She called Dad, who was almost as shook up as she was. As it turned out, I didn't play the rest of that year, but by the time next season started they had forgotten about making me quit hockey.

Anyway, by my last year with the TeePees Dad had become a fan and was just as anxious as I that I make good in hockey. I gave him tickets to all the home games and right away he became an authority.

"What happened to you guys last night?" he'd ask. "You really got outskated. And what's the matter with you? You must have been asleep. Why else would you pass the puck off when you had an open net?" And so on. An instant expert—which may be one of the reasons hockey's such a great spectator sport, a new fan gets involved extra fast.

Mom and he were unhappy, however, that I had stopped going to school in Grade 11, when I turned eighteen. Pilous had switched practice from afternoons to mornings and at first, I just cut the morning classes. After a while, I stopped attending in the afternoon, too, instead going to shows with buddies like McKenzie or Ravlich. School, which had been easy, had become a chore, so I quit.

The Link Is Formed / 49

Dad was angry at first. "Why in hell do you think I'm working this hard?" he asked. "It's to put you through school. I promised your mother when she let us take you to get you through school. You've got some brains. You could become a lawyer or a professional man and you can't be sure how hockey will turn out. Even if you're successful, you could be hurt and that would be the end of it. Then what would you do for a living?" But he just talked. He never pushed or forced me to anything so I quit school.

In the summer of 1959 there was no longer any doubt in my mind that I wanted to turn pro. Other players with not nearly as good Junior records were playing in the NHL. I wasn't as big as some of them, but that hadn't stopped me at St. Catharines. I had been able to keep up with them and, according to some of the newspaper stories I was reading, had been able to do better than quite a few. I still wanted to prove myself, to show I was as good as anybody. I know one thing: the favorable notices in the press hadn't given me a big head. I may have seemed cocky, sure of myself, but beneath that chippy exterior I was just as uncertain as ever whether I really belonged. I just wasn't letting on.

Most of all, I wasn't about to let on to Tommy Ivan, general manager of the Black Hawks. I didn't want him to think I undervalued myself because if I was going to turn pro, I wanted to make sure it meant something. I was going to make those press clippings and the scoring championship pay off in good hard cash.

The first time I sat down with Ivan I hardly knew the man. I was to learn in later years and countless hours of contract negotiations just how tough a bargainer he could be. It got to be almost fun, a game. But the first time we talked, in the fall of 1959, I was just a green kid, unsure of myself, but desperately determined to get a fair shake from a shrewd, experienced hockey executive.

I had received a letter in the summer inviting me to the Black Hawk training camp that fall, held in St. Catharines in those days. Other than that letter, I hadn't heard from Ivan, even after a couple of weeks of camp went by, giving me time to talk with Bobby Hull, as well as some of the older Hawks, about how much money I should ask for. I decided not to sign for anything less than $8,500 a year on a two-year contract. The NHL minimum was $7,500, now it's $10,000.

When it appeared in camp that I was going to make the team, Ivan called me into the office he had at the Queensway Hotel in St. Catharines. He opened the bidding: "We're prepared to pay you $7,500 if you can stick with us and we'll also sign you to a $4,000 minor-league contract in case we have to send you to Buffalo."

I shook my head: "I don't know, Mr. Ivan, that's not enough."

He knew the whole routine and just asked, "Well, what do you want?"

I said, "I want a two-year contract at $9,000 a year."

He blinked, then said softly, "My boy, we can't pay you that much. Where do you think we're going to get the money? We can't go that big with untried rookies." He had a point, but I was determined not to let him outmaneuver me.

"Mr. Ivan, I can't sign for less," I said.

"How do you know you'll make the club?" he asked.

"I don't, but I presume I will."

He tried a different approach: "What about this minor-league contract?"

I shook my head again: "That's not enough either."

I could see he was a little impatient, but he just said, "Well, let's get your National League salary straightened away first and then we'll talk about your minor-league contract. As I said, we're prepared to give you $7,500. Think it over a while."

I didn't hear from him for maybe a week, but I wasn't going to show I was worrying.

Finally, he called me: "Have you changed your mind?"

I acted nonchalant: "What about?"

I wouldn't have blamed him if he had gotten angry, but he just said, "Well, about your contract."

"No."

"Do you still want $9,000?"

"Yeah."

"Well, we'll give you $8,000."

"No." That ended that.

It went right down to the last day of camp. I was worried in one way and in another way I wasn't because I still had a year of junior eligibility. On the other hand, I was eager to prove myself as a pro. And I knew by the way I had been playing at

The Link Is Formed

camp that I had made the club, even if only as a fourth center. Ivan called me in for a last try.

"We'll give you $8,000," he said, "and that's being fair."

"I want $8,500 and a two-year contract."

He laughed a little, then said, "All right, you've got it. Now what about the minor-league contract?"

I was going to play it up to the end: "I don't think I'll play in the minors."

I could see he was amused at that when he said, "I hope you don't, but if you do we have to have something down on paper." We settled on $5,500 for the minor-league contract.

I had heard of players getting bonuses for turning pro so I wasn't afraid to ask for a little extra.

Ivan said, "We'll give you $2,000 for signing. That's fair enough."

I shook my head: "I had a little more in mind—$5,000."

Tommy bargained a little, then laughed and said, "Okay."

I came out of there feeling pretty good since I'd gotten exactly what I wanted. I thought then, and still do, that Ivan had been very fair with me. And when you think about it, that was a lot of money to a nineteen-year-old kid. I showed Dad the contract, and he thought so, too.

Dad right away wanted to make sure I didn't waste the $5,000 bonus. "That's a lot of money, son," he said. "Why don't you buy some Canadian bonds with it? There might be a time when you'll need that money. Now maybe you can go back to school in the summertime and finish up."

I agreed—but I'm still waiting to go back. I guess it would have been better if I had, but at that time I wasn't thinking about much of anything other than hockey.

I was nineteen and a pro, headed for Chicago. I couldn't want anything more.

6

Up to the Black Hawks

I DON'T KNOW if I was the cockiest kid who ever came into the league, I just suspect it. I was much like Derek Sanderson, a chippy young man who joined the Boston Bruins in 1967, but by then I was a more or less wise veteran and Derek seemed like a cocky kid to me. I figured he would learn, as I did.

In the fall of 1959 and for the next couple of years I was trying to prove I belonged in the league. It was like saying, "All right, so I am a DP and maybe you don't think I belong here, but I'm going to show you I do belong and it doesn't matter who you are, how long you've been around or how many trophies you've won."

I butt-ended with the stick, elbowed, ran at players from behind. I was a dirty player. I'm sure a lot of them hated me, but I felt I had to prove one way or the other I was going to stay in the league and nobody could run me out.

When you're a rookie everybody tests your guts. Every chance a defenseman gets he'll take a run at you just to let you know you can't mess around with him.

One of the roughest, toughest defensemen in the league when I broke in was Fernie Flaman of the Boston Bruins. He had been around quite a while and had little use for rookies, so he didn't waste much time teaching me a lesson.

I had a bad knack of admiring my own passes, turning my head to watch the puck cross the ice. This would leave me wide open for players coming on my blind side, and I'd get creamed. Lindsay, my left wing, pulled me aside once after I took a check that almost shook me loose from my brains, and said, "Look kid, before you get killed, instead of watching the puck when you pass, get that stick up about chest-high and watch for some guy coming at you, because they're going to do it for the first couple of years."

Up to the Black Hawks / 53

I tried to follow his advice, but would forget once in a while. I used to jump up a little, too, if a guy hit me against the boards, so that my shoulders and hips would take the blow against the wood.

We were playing Boston and Flaman was on the ice. I got the puck in our end and swung around to see Flaman coming at me; so I passed quickly, jumped up and put the stick in the air, just as Lindsay had suggested. I caught Flaman under the eye on the cheekbone with the stick. The cut was good for five or six stitches, but he didn't bother to go in and get sewed up. The next face-off he was standing at the point, glaring at me, the blood on his cheek. If looks could kill, I would have been dead.

Being on the spot, I couldn't let down, so I sort of laughed, telling him, "Aw, go jump in the lake you old has-been. You're not going to catch me." He didn't—not until the third period!

It was the same kind of play except I was looking back over my shoulder, having forgotten what Lindsay told me. I no sooner passed the puck than Flaman nailed me with a good, clean bodycheck. I went up in the air and came down like a load of bricks and I crawled to the bench. He had really knocked the wind out of me, that's all, but I felt like a garbage truck had run over me.

Every club seemed to have one or two defensemen who were running at me, testing me. If I made a bad play they'd sneer, "Huh, you sawdust bushleaguer, you young punk, you don't belong up here. You'll be back where you belong before you know it."

It was a long time before I was sure they were wrong, although I didn't feel insecure. At that age I didn't understand insecurity; but I knew I had to prove I belonged, that one season or two doesn't make a hockey player. I didn't particularly care how I went about it, even if I had to kick the skates out from under a few. Fans at home egged me on, too . . . they loved the rough stuff. For the first few years, being chippy tied in very much with my feeling of pride and my drive to prove myself as good as anyone or better.

It wasn't the way I had played at St. Catharines, although I didn't back off there either. But I never ran at a player from behind as a Junior, I'd go up and meet him. Most were my size or a little bigger, but not by as much as in the big league. And the juniors didn't know as many cute tricks as the NHL experts. I fought for survival.

The battle began October 7, 1959, the day the Hawks opened the season against the New York Rangers at Chicago. Rudy Pilous put me on a line centering for Bobby Hull and Eric Nesterenko, and I was lucky enough to get my first NHL goal. When I say lucky, I'm not being modest, just truthful. It wasn't a goal to be proud of, although I dove into the net to get the puck for a souvenir. Bobby shot the puck and it hit me in the behind, bouncing past Gump Worsley, the Rangers goalie. A real "garbage" goal!

Pilous hadn't wasted much breath on what he expected of me as a rookie. "Just go out there and play your game," he said. "I know what you can do, and you know what you can do. Don't forget that you'll never stop learning. You might get one deke down to a fine science but you can only pull it once or twice a game. You have to keep trying different variations, surprise the others as often as you can."

This is what I did the first year, watching the other players, mostly the centers on the other teams, the men I was playing against directly. You learn after a while what another man can do best, whether he can hook check, poke check or play your body most of the time.

Things didn't go well at the start, and Pilous put the "Million Dollar Line" together, with Bobby at left wing, Bill Hay at center and Murray Balfour on the right. I moved to a line with Lindsay and Kenny Wharram. Lindsay was nearing the end of a great career and was of tremendous help to a youngster. As for Kenny, it was the beginning of a long association with him, which after a while turned into a great friendship.

That first season was more of a learning period for me than anything else. I scored only eight goals, with eighteen assists, and for a while wondered if I would be farmed out to Buffalo. We were a man over the cutdown limit, and when the time came I was surprised they farmed out Phil Maloney, a veteran center. The difference probably was his age, since he was thirty-two while I was nineteen and the Hawks were trying to build up the team with youngsters. I really wouldn't have minded going to Buffalo at the time because I thought the experience would do me good; I would be getting more ice time and learning more. After the second year I thought it fortunate I hadn't been sent down; I discovered I could learn more

Up to the Black Hawks / 55

in the NHL by watching and practicing, and maybe working a little harder than some others, than I could have learned in the minors.

The things I learned weren't confined to hockey. I found new and lasting friendships and discovered the perils of being on my own in the big city.

I was closest to Bobby, Ron Murphy, and Tod Sloan at the start, since we shared a two-bedroom apartment in Berwyn, a western suburb, that first winter. (Most Chicago players live west of the city because the rink is near the major east-west expressway.) Bobby and I were in one room, Murphy and Sloan in the other. We even shared a car, putting up fifty dollars total to buy a ten-year-old jalopy. It had a hole in the floor that we plugged with cardboard, and the heater didn't work, but it got us to the Stadium. Bobby and I were single and we ran around together. Murphy and Sloan were married but didn't have their families with them.

Sloan and Earl Balfour liked to go out to the racetrack and I'd trail along. I didn't know much about horses but Tod and Earl did and explained things. I also didn't know much about the kind of people who hung around tracks, and it cost me $1,000 to find out about touts. I had just cashed two paychecks, and I had that much on me when I went to the track with Tod and Earl.

One reason we went that day was because Count Swedak, a horse belonging to Jim Norris, was running. Norris owned the Black Hawks and Sloan knew him, although I didn't. Sloan also knew Norris' runner, the man he sent from his box to the mutuel windows to place bets. Sloan would watch for the runner to leave Norris' box, stop him and find out what Jim was betting, then bet the same way. We got word that things looked good for Count Swedak in the third race. I backed him with $50, the most money I'd ever bet in my life. Darned if Count Swedak didn't come in and pay 3-1, letting me collect $200.

I bet just $5 the next couple of races, figuring to be smart and go home a winner. I was walking away from the mutuel window when a little man stopped me and asked, "Don't I know you from someplace?" I was impressed. Here it was my first year in the league in a city of three and a half million people and I was recognized.

I said, "I don't know, you might have seen me play hockey. I play for the Chicago Black Hawks."

He smiled, saying, "Yeah, I thought I recognized you. I'm a former jockey. See my buddy over there?" He pointed to the tout he was working with who had a stack of $5 mutuel win tickets three or four inches high.

I was impressed, thinking they really knew the horses. "Listen, do you want to make some dough?" he asked.

I nodded.

"How much money you got on you?"

I told him I had around $1,000. "Well, give me a few bucks and we'll play the same horse. He can't lose. The only way he can lose is if he breaks a leg or if they shoot him."

I gave him $800 and he gave me the tickets. They were legitimate so I didn't suspect anything and the nag went off at 3–2. The horse broke beautifully from the gate, was leading three-fourths of the way around when all of a sudden—I figured somebody shot him because he just died, finishing sixth. I saw my little friend after the race and I gestured, as if to ask, "What happened?"

He said, "Did you see the son of a gun step in the hole?" I didn't want to appear stupid, so I nodded.

"Don't worry, we'll get even," he said. "What do you have left?" So I gave him the rest of my money and lost that, too. I was out $1,000.

When Sloan and Balfour found out what had happened they nearly died laughing and told me they couldn't believe I was that stupid. For a while they wouldn't let me out of their sight in case I got lost.

I got set straight in other ways as a rookie. It's a good time to learn humility. Teammates treated rookies in the NHL like college fraternity pledges in old TV movies, but with a sense of fun. There were three of us newcomers in the club in 1959, Bill Hay and Murray Balfour were the other two. The veterans literally shaved our heads and played a few other practical jokes on us, but the main thing was that they regarded us as errand boys.

If we were going someplace in a car, I had to do the driving. After the last exhibition game at Sault Ste. Marie, I chauffered Glenn Hall, our goalie, to Chicago. After we bought the old clunker, it was my job to drive it like a taxi.

I was always running errands. If we were on the road and had twenty minutes to catch a train, the veterans would jump in a cab, give me a couple of empty suitcases they lugged

Up to the Black Hawks / 57

around for that purpose, and say, "Okay, kid, go fill 'em up with beer." They'd hold the cab until I ran to the nearest liquor store, bought a couple of cases of cold beer, and put them in the suitcases. I could hardly lift them, being the smallest in the bunch, but I had to tote them, and I swear that's how I developed my arm muscles. What's worse, I'd end up paying for the beer because they'd never pay me back. That was just part of a rookie's fee.

I suppose veterans felt rookies were a threat to their jobs, but they never showed it in conversation or in any other way off the ice. A veteran who felt threatened might work just that much harder on the ice. He might play a practical joke on you, but wouldn't take it out on you in another way.

When it came to a game situation, it was all for one and one for all. The veterans didn't give a hoot who scored the goals or how they were scored as long as everybody was helping the team. When you didn't do your share, they let you know. Sure, the young kid coming up at that time was hazed, but if you went along with what was expected, if you did your job, you could get in with them, you could belong. I may be getting older, but I think the veterans then liked rookies better and felt closer to them than they do now.

I can't say that being chippy on the ice, much as it helped me stay in the league, helped me with my coach or teammates. I was frequently in the penalty box and the team had to work harder, playing a man short while killing penalties and at that time it was the full two minutes. You didn't come out of the penalty box the moment the other team scored, you stayed in for two minutes even if the opposition scored three goals. I ran up 119 penalty minutes that first year in sixty-four games, missing six games because of a broken wrist.

Pilous finally said something after a stretch in which I was getting too many misconducts and stupid penalties such as hooking and holding, the kind that result from not skating hard enough.

"First of all, I don't have anything to say about your play," he said. "I think you're doing all right there, but cut out the stupid, idiotic penalties you've been getting. See if you can learn to keep your mouth shut. Quit yapping at the officials."

It took me a little while to learn how to put a lock on my mouth. Whenever I or one of my teammates got a penalty, although I didn't have an "A" (for alternate captain) on my shirt, I'd swear or holler at the referee. It seems to me now that the referees then were a little more tolerant and shut their ears, otherwise I could have had twice as many misconduct penalties as I did the first year. But I got in a bad enough scrape for all that, although it wasn't intentional.

Referee Vern Buffey had called a penalty on me and I charged him. I didn't mean to hit him, but ran towards him, meaning to stop. I tripped over something and fell, catching him across the body with my stick. He gave me a game misconduct and the next time we were in Montreal I was to see Clarence Campbell, president of the NHL, for a hearing. I had never met Campbell and was scared to death. I hadn't meant to hit Buffey but it had happened. I was sorry for it, but I could have injured him seriously if I had hit him in the head with the stick. Luckily, I didn't have to go to the hearing alone. Ed Litzenberger, as captain of the team, and Ted Lindsay went to Campbell's office with me. Teddy had been in a few scrapes of his own and said, "I'd better go with you, kid. You might need some help and might not be able to express yourself the way you want to." Litzenberger wanted to make sure none of his players was mistreated. I guess because I was so young, Campbell didn't object to Litzenberger and Lindsay coming with me. I don't know whether Litz and Lindsay being there helped, but luckily Campbell let me off with a $300 fine and a warning. I was a little more careful with referees after that.

At the end of that first year I didn't feel that I had done badly; I had a lot to learn, but after all I was just turning twenty. I could stick-handle and I could pass the puck, my two big assets. My weaknesses were checking and skating. I had to work on keeping up with the others. I never was a fast skater and I dipsy-doodled too much instead of taking off with the puck. At that time, I was trying to beat the same player four times. What I mean is that I'd beat him in our end zone, at the blue line, at the red line and also at their blue line because I was skating laterally as much as forward. I also had a tendency to leave my check too soon. Let's say, Wharram was caught back in their end zone. I would pick up his check but I wouldn't stay with him long enough. The puck was like a magnet to me, I would go back and chase it, leaving the opposing winger I was guarding wide open. As soon as I left my check, the man with the puck would slip it over to him and he would

Up to the Black Hawks / 59

either get a good shot on net or score. Fact is, I think I still have the same fault, but not as much.

I had a lot to learn, but fortunately I had friends to help me along. There was Bobby, of course, only a year and a half older, but already one of the biggest names in hockey. He scored thirty-nine goals that season and led the league in scoring with eighty-one points.

And there were Glenn Hall and his wife Pauline. I don't think I've ever met a sweeter woman in my life—other than my wife and mother and two daughters, naturally. She was almost a house-mother to the kids on the team. If Bobby had to be away some place, the Halls would invite me over to dinner. I'd help Pauline with the dishes, and perhaps we would discuss some things that were bothering me. She'd always give me a fresh point of view.

If I had some sort of personal problem, I'd talk it over with Glenn. He'd straighten me out, being a lot older and more experienced, having been around and through his own tough times. Glenn was quiet with crowds, but if you got him off on his own he was different. He seemed to know a little something about everything, and in a funny way, he was never wrong—anyway, he never admitted being wrong. It became a sort of standing joke on the team that if you wanted to know something, you'd ask Glenn Hall and whatever he said was law.

In that first year, Glenn and I struck up a wonderful friendship. I still consider Pauline and Glenn, as well as Kenny Wharram and his wife, Jean, among my closest friends, although I didn't get to know the Wharrams well until later.

That rookie year opened a lot of doors to me, not the least a chance to return to Czechoslovakia in the summer of 1960 for my first visit since I had left in 1948. You can imagine how emotional that family reunion was. But more about that later. The three months in the old country were wonderful, but I soon was eager to start the next hockey season.

7

It Pays to Win

WE WERE a young and willing team and that had a lot to do with winning the Stanley Cup in the 1960–61 season, the first time the Black Hawks had done it in twenty-three years. It's easy to sit back and scoff about spirit, saying it's something writers invent, that it has little or nothing to do with winning games, scoring goals or making sure the other team doesn't score. Not that I would say success depends on having a set amount of spirit and another percentage of ability, because you can't divide the two things so neatly. But spirit is important, more than you realize at times.

I've known men without great ability who just by sheer guts have gone out and proved the point that they belonged in the NHL. Reggie Fleming was one of them. When he came to us in the fall of 1960 he wasn't a polished hockey player at all; he was a less than ordinary skater and his shot wasn't the greatest in the world. But he helped us win that Stanley Cup and he did it more with spirit than with ability.

It was Bill Hay who said, "Reggie's most effective when you keep him cold." In other words, you left Reggie on the bench almost the whole game, then brought him on when you needed somebody fresh, somebody to give the team a lift, a spark.

Along the years, Fleming improved his skill as a player through sheer effort. I'm sure he had a little help along the way, but if Reggie hadn't been the conscientious fellow that he was he wouldn't have progressed as much. If he couldn't shoot, he'd work on his shot. If he couldn't skate, he'd stay out on the ice in practice and skate longer than anybody else. This effort, this refusal to give in is part of what I call spirit. And it had a lot to do with our being able to win the Stanley Cup in my second year with the Hawks.

On paper, we had no business beating Montreal in the first round of the playoffs. Canadiens were the powerhouse, with players like Jean Beliveau, Henri Richard, Dickie Moore, Boom Boom Geoffrion, Doug Harvey and Jacques Plante, to name just a few. But we had momentum going for us toward the end of the season and carried it on into the playoffs. We knew we could beat Detroit in the finals if we beat Montreal in the first round, and beating Detroit figured to be sort of anticlimactic. When I talk about momentum, I mean that everybody on the team was playing well, everybody was contributing 100% to the effort whether it was checking or scoring goals. We didn't expect certain players to score, but we did expect each one to check. We expected them all not to have a goal scored against them, and it turned out that way in the last two games with Montreal, both of which we won 3–0. The defensemen were playing defense, the forwards were playing both ways, offensively and defensively, and of course we had tremendous goalkeeping from Glenn Hall.

I've heard it said that every goal scored is the result of three mistakes, maybe four: bad forechecking, bad defense crossing the center line, bad play at the blue line, and maybe bad goaltending. Most of the time this is true. But once in a while there's a good play on the part of the other team or by an individual player on it that results in a goal and you can't point to a real mistake made by any member of the team that has been scored on. I've seen a defenseman make the best possible play that he could and yet have an opposing player go in to score. Fortunately, in those final two games at Montreal, we didn't make any of the three or four mistakes and they didn't make that superb play that can result in a goal without a mistake on the part of the defense.

Before the season started Rudy Pilous, our coach, made another of the decisions that influenced the whole course of my hockey career. During the summer Ted Lindsay had retired and Wharram and I were without a left wing. In training camp, Pilous put us together with Ab McDonald, who had been obtained along with Fleming and several others in a complicated nine-player deal that summer. We seemed to hit it off perfectly together from the start; the Scooter Line had been formed. I guess Tommy Ivan gave us the name because, he said, "they scoot around so much on the ice."

McDonald, then twenty-four, was from Winnipeg, Manitoba. He had played for the St. Catharines Junior-A team a few years before I had, then moved on to Rochester in the

American Hockey League before being called up to the Montreal Canadiens in 1958. He played two seasons with the Canadiens, then was sold to the Hawks. Later on, after being sent to Boston in the trade for Doug Mohns in 1964, he bounced around a bit, but was a valuable member of the St. Louis Blues in 1968–69 when they won the Western Division title and lost out to the Canadiens in the Stanley Cup finals.

Ab was our leader. He had an inventive mind and was always willing to try something new. Kenny and I had a few plays which we had set up the year before with Lindsay, but we didn't use them that much. When McDonald joined us, he took charge. He made sure that practice was used to best advantage.

When we had line rushes, he'd get us together in a corner and say, "Instead of going up the ice doing nothing, let's try some plays even if we never use them in a game. Let's say we're in a situation where the three of us are breaking on two defensemen or even two-on-one. Let's make sure we know exactly what each of us is going to do, where he's going to be without even looking."

These are the things we worked on with Ab. All it needed was a little holler from one of us to indicate that he was open. We still do that. I know exactly where Wharram is going to be 90% of the time and this is a big advantage because you might have your back to the play. We've scored a lot of goals like that. I might be going away from the net and hear a voice hollering "Kita!" and I know just what to do.

We started using the play in which when the other team's defenseman had the puck behind the net one of us would play his body and the other would pick up the puck. This is almost a standard play now, but like the others we had to learn it for ourselves.

McDonald also made me think about a lot of things that I hadn't realized before.

"If you get into this position," he'd say, pointing to a spot on the ice, "it doesn't matter if I'm wide open around the net because I'm in perfect position for a rebound. So don't pass, shoot instead. Let me go for the rebound."

It was sensible to figure the player near the net was always in a better position than I was, so the thing to do was pass the puck to him. I hadn't thought so much about anticipating the

It Pays to Win / 63

rebound as a play in itself or the fact that his angle on the side of the net might be worse than mine.

McDonald set up specific plays for almost every situation.

"Let's try the drop pass to Kenny right over the blue line," he'd say. "Just as soon as you get across the blue line and cut across, drop the puck to Kenny and he can fire it to me real quick. I'll either take a slap shot or a wrist shot and you'll be in position to tip it in or get the rebound."

Ab and I were close. We'd go out to long three-hour lunches after practice and, while having a few beers, we'd work out new plays on a piece of paper. Then we'd ask Kenny about it and get his views. At that time Kenny preferred to go home for lunch although we'd get together on the road. It wasn't until the year after we won the Stanley Cup that Ken and I became the firm friends we have been since.

Just about everything I do now dates back from the first Scooter line. Being the center, I was the playmaker. Starting off, the defenseman would pass the puck up either to one side, to Ab or Ken, or up the middle, to me. Our big play was "coming from behind." Ab and I would throw the puck back and forth a couple of times until we hit the center-ice red line or just outside their blue line. If I could carry the puck inside the blue line, I would rag it a few moments until Kenny came busting in on the right. By then he had at least a step or more on his check, and if the defenseman went with me, Kenny was open and I could slide the puck to him. If the defenseman went back with him, I could move in and either take a shot or give the puck back to Ab. This was a basic play and we had a lot of variations on it, including the drop pass, which a lot of lines later copied from us. I know that New York's line of Rod Gilbert, Jean Ratelle, and Vic Hadfield play almost the same style we used.

Of course, in 1960–61, we were just working out these things and none of us had that big a year. I had nineteen goals and thirty-four assists, Ab had seventeen goals, and Kenny had sixteen. But I also had the first sustained scoring streak of my career and for the first time got a taste of what it felt like to get some real newspaper attention.

I scored ten goals in an eight-game stretch from late December, 1960, through mid-January, 1961. Since the Hawks put together a seven-game winning streak in that time, matching the longest they had ever had, my spurt meant something more than just personal achievement. And it made it easier because when you're winning, things seem to fall into place.

All I remember about the streak is the ninth game against Toronto, when I was trying to tie the record for consecutive games scored in. It's the first time I ever felt real pressure, and I couldn't sleep the night before the game. In the game, it seemed to me that I got fifty shots on goal, but I couldn't get anything past Johnny Bower, the Toronto goaltender. Maybe they were checking me closely because I was hot, but I'm sure they weren't keeping an eye on me as much as they have in recent years. The Leafs must have been conscious of my going for the record, though. I know that our coach, when a guy on another team is hot, tells us to watch him a little closer than usual, because when a man is going like that, he can be shooting from outside the blue line and the puck is liable to bounce off somebody's skate and go in.

That seven-game streak might have given us a little extra confidence. Anyway, it helped us finish in third place and we went into the playoffs feeling pretty good, although Montreal had beaten us in four straight games in the first round the year before. But we were a different club in a lot of ways than in 1959–60. For one thing, we were a little rougher; Fleming and Murray Balfour didn't back off from anybody. In fact, we'd been involved in a couple of good rows during the season.

The biggest rhubarb was when Pierre Pilote, our little defenseman, hit Eddie Shack of the Maple Leafs over the head with his stick at Toronto. Before it ended, Murray Balfour was chasing Carl Brewer of the Leafs up the ice, threatening to kill him, and other Hawk players were in the stands, fighting fans sitting behind our bench. Even Dick Shatto, the Toronto Argonauts football player, who was a spectator, came out of the stands and started after Balfour. Before it was over, four policemen had to break up the brawl and afterward referee Frank Udvari's penalty calls resulted in $725 in fines.

But that's the kind of club we were, full of fight, and we weren't about to turn into angels when we opened the semifinals with the Canadiens at Montreal. They won the first game 6–3 and we came back in the second game to win 4–3 with Eddie Litzenberger getting the big goal; but it was the third game, March 26, 1961, in Chicago that decided the series.

That's one game I'll never forget. It was a close-checking contest but there were enough chances on both sides to score,

It Pays to Win / 65

although we had just a 1–0 lead going into the last minute of play. That's when I got into a fight with Bill Hicke and both of us went to the penalty box, getting two minutes each for roughing. We started fighting again in the penalty box so the referee gave us five minutes more plus a ten-minute misconduct each. That was seventeen minutes in penalties and the referee "suggested" we might as well go down to the dressing rooms. All right, I figured we had the game won. So I went downstairs to the dressing room, then started taking off my uniform. Suddenly there was this tremendous shout, although I didn't know what it was about until my teammates charged into the room. With a half minute left, Henri Richard had scored the tying goal for the Canadiens and we were going into a twenty-minute "sudden death" overtime.

"Kid, you'd better get dressed," said Pilous. "We might need you."

So I got into a clean uniform and went upstairs when the first overtime period started. I didn't think I'd play, since I still had most of that seventeen minutes in penalties left and I thought surely somebody would score a goal before that. I came out with three minutes to go but no one scored in the first overtime, although Donnie Marshall hit our goal post with a shot and we hit their post twice. In the second overtime, Dickie Moore's shot hit the post, then one of our players deked their goaltender but just missed the corner of the net with his shot.

In the third overtime, Montreal got a penalty. Although I was playing right point on the power play, I somehow ended up on the left side and the puck came out to me. I wound up for a slap shot and half-fanned on it. I got just enough of the puck to get in past the first Canadien, who was charging into me, and it reached Murray Balfour, who was standing in front of the net. He just wheeled around with a backhand shot and put the puck through the goalie's legs. That was the game and actually the series. Those three overtimes really sapped the Canadiens. I know it sapped us, too, but the difference was that we won the game. They won the next game, but it really didn't matter. We just knew we would beat them in the series and we did, Glenn Hall shutting them out the next two games. A remarkable feat.

The final with the Red Wings went six games but we never thought the outcome was in doubt. Once we had defeated

Montreal the major part of the job was done. Not that Detroit didn't give us a battle, right into the last game. They were leading 1–0 in the sixth game when Reggie Fleming, who played a helluva game for us that night, scored a short-handed goal. It was the turning point. If the Red Wings had scored, it would have been 2–0; but Reggie had made it 1–1, and when McDonald put us ahead with a goal on which Kenny and I assisted we were able to control the game. By the time Eric Nesterenko put in the fifth goal for us in the third period, we knew it was all over.

You really can't explain the jubilation that goes with winning a Stanley Cup. It's not the money. Pride of achievement has a lot to do with it. Sticks and gloves went up in the air at the final buzzer and the boys jumped over the boards, picked up Glenn Hall and carried him bodily off the Detroit Olympia ice.

Our victory party has to be one of the longest on record. We started at the airport in Detroit and really got rolling when owners Jim Norris and Mike Wirtz came into the bar and said, "Give the boys whatever they want." Somebody grabbed Wirtz's hat and we started drinking champagne out of it. There was snow in Detroit and snow in Chicago and we finally got word that all flights had been cancelled. Norris called up the old Leland Hotel and rented a ballroom and we continued the party until about five in the morning. Few of us got to bed because the flight to Chicago left at 8 A.M. When we arrived in Chicago a mob of Black Hawk fans was waiting at O'Hare Field. We got a siren escort down to the Loop, a parade, and a speech from Mayor Richard Daley in which he called us the "greatest hockey team ever put together any place in this world." That night we continued the party in the lobby of the Palace Theater, which Norris and Wirtz had taken over for the occasion.

I'm not much of a champagne drinker, preferring beer, but I would have enjoyed a few more victory parties like that one. We had just one other big celebration—when we finished in first place in 1966–67—which meant something special because the Hawks had never done it before in their forty-year history. But even the joy of that was blunted because we were eliminated in the first round of the playoffs.

In one way, 1960–61 was the only completely satisfying year from a team standpoint that we had. We weren't ex-

It Pays to Win / 67

pected to win the Stanley Cup but we surprised everybody and did. In the following seasons it was the other way around. We were expected to finish in first place and win the playoffs but with the exception of 1966–67, we did neither. People began saying we couldn't take the pressure and that we folded. They couldn't understand how a team with players like Bobby Hull, Pierre Pilote, Glenn Hall and Kenny Wharram—not to mention a few others with great ability who didn't get as much ink—could miss finishing on top. I don't really know, maybe we were overrated. One thing is sure—if we all had been as good as the fans thought we were, we would have been first. But we weren't, and when we tore up the league for most of the 1962–63 season and then lost out near the end, it cost Rudy Pilous his job. Billy Reay, who had been coaching at Buffalo, took over the club for the 1963–64 season.

I don't want to give anybody the idea these were bad years. They were good for both the club and me because we always got into the playoffs where you could make a little extra money. Personally, I was doing fairly well, getting a few more goals and assists each year, even leading the league in scoring in 1963–64 and 1964–65. Starting with the 1961–62 season, I averaged over eighty points a year for the next eight seasons, which meant I must have been doing my job as a center.

It's hard to pick out any one reason for the steady point-total improvement. I think when you're starting out, you're a bit reluctant to try new things. I felt this way in practice, although at first at training camp I would go all out, hit anybody that was coming near me because I wanted to make the club. After I had made it, I didn't want to jump at my teammates in the corners. What was the sense? Why hurt the guy or yourself when you're fighting for the same cause? It took me a while to get over this reluctance to try new things.

Then there's the matter of confidence or mental attitude. It has a lot to do with the way you play and perform. I know that the first year I didn't have as much confidence as in the second, the third, the fourth, and so on. Also, you get a little stronger as you get older. And the guys on your team, the style of play, the number of good scoring chances you get in a game are all important in how well you do.

Ab McDonald kept pointing this out to me. Good old Ab! "Don't feel you're playing badly because you're not scoring goals," he would say. "Start feeling bad when you're not getting the chances, when you're not getting the shots on net."

That has been true. Some days the goals go in like buckets of water, the next day you couldn't put the puck in the ocean.

Confidence, or being mentally "right," is the key. Take stick-handling. During the 1968–69 season, it seemed something happened to me when I was carrying the puck. Maybe playing with those foot injuries, and the back injury that forced me to wear a brace, hampered my maneuverability. Anyhow, once I deked past a player there was a feeling in me that I might not beat the next guy, that I'd better pass off to somebody who could go a little faster. When I'm right, I keep the puck a little longer, beating the second man and maybe even the third. By that time I'm usually in a good position to shoot. But because I lacked confidence, one of the plays that we used quite often wasn't working the way it should. After getting across the blue line with Kenny coming up on my right, I would fake a drop pass to him and just wind up and let go with a slap shot or use a wrist shot. I began doing it even when I was off balance and the shot wouldn't break an egg shell.

I'd think, "Maybe my shot is slipping a little." But if I had had enough confidence, I wouldn't have taken the shot while off balance. I would have righted myself or done something else with the puck. When you have confidence, doing the right thing comes naturally, almost without thinking.

In the early years, as my scoring went up so did my confidence. Being picked for the All-Star teams didn't hurt and setting a scoring record with twenty-one points on six goals and fifteen assists in the 1961–62 playoffs also gave me a boost. I had a few hat tricks, too, and began getting more and more notice in the newspapers and magazines. Sure, I liked reading about myself in one way, but in another way I didn't give a hoot; I didn't always care for the way the writers approached the game. Let's say I scored two or three goals in a game and fellows like Bill Hay, Eric Nesterenko, and Chico Maki had killed off the penalties and actually saved the game for us. I thought they deserved the credit, the big writeup, because that's what the game is basically about, not letting the opposition score.

Still, I have to admit there were times when I might have been getting a big head. I was young and it may have been natural that the publicity started working on me. I suppose I thought I wouldn't be getting all this ink if I wasn't pretty good. But thinking about the other guys on the club helped me to keep my feet on the ground, although I'd be a liar to say I didn't have a big head at one time, maybe even without knowing it. However, when I started to get up too high, somebody would shoot me down, and nobody ever did it as well as my wife, Jill. After I met her in 1962 and we were married on April 27, 1963, there was no chance of my letting things go to my head. Jill hates a phony and isn't shy about expressing her opinions. If I got to thinking that I was better than others, she wasted no time in setting me straight.

8

Le Petit Diable

I'VE BEEN CALLED a lot of choice names, most of them unprintable, because of my style during the first seven years of my National Hockey League career. In Montreal, the French Canadians called me *Le Petit Diable*. That probably fit because I *was* sort of a little devil. Raising hell on the ice in order to come home a winner was part of my game. One writer even suggested that if my hockey stick had turned into the devil's pitchfork, it would have gone perfectly well with my red and black uniform.

I was rough, and sometimes downright mean, in the heat of banging around on the ice with thousands of people either howling for my blood or urging me on. At first, I felt I had to use every means at my disposal in order to survive in a league filled with talented, bigger men where you were always being tested. We also come back to that "trying harder" philosophy of mine, and maybe some of my efforts were misdirected. Chalk up some of these things to immaturity. Once you get a reputation for being a tough guy, you feel you just can't ever show the slightest sign of giving an inch or backing down—almost like a teenager's game of "chicken," which proves nothing about being a strong individual or a he-man.

I might even have felt it was the only way to make sure I could stay on top. I figured a chip on my shoulder was as essential a piece of equipment as my stick—and I use all my equipment. If that style brought me to where I was, what would happen without it? When I joined the NHL I'd heard about many players who came into the league with more ability than I had at the same stage, and guys would take two or three runs at them . . . and chase them right out of the league. I didn't want this to happen to me. Then, too, when I became known as a scorer and playmaker, I had to retaliate and hand it back or I'd be a target for every elbow, knee and stick in the league. This is a hard fact of life in any rugged body-contact sport—the more you achieve, the more personal attention you get from the opposition.

Some of my tactics were designed to needle someone into reacting and drawing a penalty—giving us the extra player and a better chance to score. I'll still do this on occasion, as do most of the other players in the NHL.

Was I a dirty player? I have to say that at times I very definitely was. It didn't take much to provoke me, and call it a fiery nature or whatever—I'd strike back any way I could and to hell with the consequences. I'm still capable of doing something dirty if I'm provoked far enough. Maybe most players wouldn't admit they're ever dirty. But, let's face it, anyone is capable of reacting or retaliating in a less than sportsmanlike way—giving a guy the butt-end of the stick, a good elbow in the guts, kneeing, running at a player from behind, spearing. When you stop to think about it, anything against the rules can be called dirty hockey, even some of those penalties like hooking and tripping that seem to be a basic, routine part of the game.

Am I denying the reputation I had? No, that was me all right and I earned it. The records show that in my first eight seasons I spent 755 minutes in the penalty box, the equivalent of more than a dozen games. And my name was in the record book under "most penalty minutes, one season, by a center." That was 1964–65, when I had 154 minutes. Even so I couldn't have been all that bad or I wouldn't have lived so long or the league office would have stepped in. Some of the writers undoubtedly helped create my reputation by turning in "interesting" copy. Nobody wants to read about just another hockey player; every story needs a good angle.

Can't say I won a lot of friends around the league, and I know I built up quite a few rivalries. I prefer to call them rivalries although some people might think of them as feuds. I don't like to use the word feud, because it implies the scraps that took place in the rink left ill-feeling that carried over into situations off the ice. I don't believe that in my case they ever did.

I can't think of one player in the league I hated off the ice. Normally, when you sit down and have a beer with another hockey player all the scraps and tangles you've had with him on the ice are forgotten. Take Eddie Shack, who played for

New York, Toronto and Boston. I was never very fond of him on the ice and I'm sure he felt the same way about me. Maybe Eddie and I would never become the greatest of friends, but when I sat down with him over a beer, we'd talk about golf, football or anything other than hockey. Just once in a while we might get a little sentimental, swapping memories.

For example: "Do you remember the time I cross-checked you in the corner and they had to peel you off the boards?" or, "I'll never forget the time I speared you and Doc had to use a sewing machine to close the cut." But as long as serious injury doesn't result from an incident on the ice, it's quickly forgotten and never brought up outside the arena.

My three main rivalries were with Henri Richard of the Canadiens, Bob Pulford of the Maple Leafs, and Lou Fontinato, a defenseman for New York and Montreal in my early NHL years.

The one with Richard went back to his older brother Maurice, the famous "Rocket." My first year was the Rocket's last, and from the beginning I used to go at Henri every game. The Rocket didn't like this, maybe because he was looking out for his kid brother, who didn't need that much looking after. After the Rocket retired, he always sat behind our bench at the Forum in Montreal and yelled at me in French and broken English, "Hey, you DP, why do you do that? What's the matter you foreigner, maybe you don't know how to play hockey?" Once he even threw a cup full of a soft drink at me. He was a fiery guy on or off the ice and when he blew his top there were fireworks aplenty. At the time, I hated his guts but later we became good friends.

I really don't know why he got on my back so much in my early years. Maybe it was partly because of my tangles with Henri and the fact that I had scored a goal or two in the Montreal Forum. Just as likely, it might have been because he missed playing hockey. There wasn't much he could do while sitting in the stands. At least, if he had been on the ice he could have felt he was part of the game and he also might have been able to do something about me.

The rivalry with Henri Richard mostly just happened. We both were fairly small compared with the other fellows, were both centers, played against each other almost every shift on the ice and always were trying to outdo each other. It started

Le Petit Diable

out as a friendly rivalry but one night we collided, came up swinging, and ever after that it was a dog-eat-dog kind of thing. In recent years it has cooled off, probably because we've both matured, but for the first three or four seasons we had some hot scraps.

One reason for our battles could have been that I had that chip on my shoulder then and felt like fighting, even though I lost ten or fifteen major fights and had only a couple of draws. Henri was my lone victim. I don't know exactly what touched it off, but we started out front and center and there were a couple of other fights going on at the same time so the linesmen didn't get between us right away to break it up. I started twirling Henri around and got in a few solid punches. By the time the linesmen stepped in we were both so tired that I was glad they broke it up. That was the time Henri set me off laughing with his "don' speak so good da Engleesh" routine.

Bobby Pulford and I have had a little "thing" going ever since I broke into the league. Sometimes it burst into open warfare, although he was taller and had a fifteen- or twenty-pound weight advantage. Whenever I would play the point on a power play, Bobby would usually take a run at me. I'd shoot the puck and still be watching its flight when he would barrel into me. Every chance I had to hit him after that I did. But the rivalry with Pulford was never as serious as the ones with Richard and Fontinato.

Fontinato never was a dirty player toward me, although a lot of guys thought he bent the rules more than he should have. Usually he would run at me with a good body or shoulder check. Once in a while his elbow or stick would come up, but not too often.

Foiling Fontinato became a challenge, especially when he ran at me. I knew I couldn't knock him down, so if I saw him coming I'd fake as if I were going to run into him. Then I'd either drop down, jump up in the air, or go sideways, and he would hit the boards. I got more satisfaction out of that than I would have from knocking him down.

I also put "Leaping Lou's" rushes to good use. He'd play the left side on defense, which would be Kenny Wharram's side as my right winger. While Kenny was breaking in from behind, I'd give Louie a couple of shifts and he'd sometimes run fifty feet at me. It's easy to beat a player that way. You give him a couple of fakes with the head, depending on which way he's going, then just go the other way to beat him. So when Louie would take a long run at me, I'd give him the shift and skate by, with Kenny busting in and home free.

Still, there's no doubt Louie didn't always miss nailing me and that he could get under my skin as well as raise a few lumps on top of it. In the playoffs one year, he made me so mad that I rushed at him down the ice and fired the puck right at his head. Luckily, I missed.

As many times as I did get into scrapes when I was *Le Petit Diable,* I think most of the time it was in retaliation for something someone else had done to me. Only twice have I ever hurt anybody without having a good reason. I hit Bill Hicke when he was with the Canadiens and I don't remember why. Another time I speared Billy Harris of Toronto, who never hit a player in his life. I don't know exactly why I did it. It was just one of those stupid things a person does, and I felt sorry afterwards.

Maybe the reason I went after Harris was because I couldn't get even with Terry Sawchuk, who was the Toronto goalie in that game. Earlier, while I had been skating by the net, Sawchuk took a swipe at me with his stick, spearing me. I went down like a ton of bricks. It knocked the wind out of me and it left a scrape on my stomach. I never had the opportunity to retaliate. Besides, you don't fight with goaltenders. I couldn't get at Sawchuk, so I guess Harris was the closest target.

I know that long before I stopped going out of my way to get someone, I'd quit drawing the cheap penalties—the hookings, holdings and the trippings. Getting those kind of penalties mostly means you're lazy and not skating, or are short on talent. You try to get away with something you shouldn't. In other words, I would go in on a guy, and if I missed him with a body check and he was getting away from me, then I'd trip him. This is a cheap penalty. I stopped taking those early.

What it really comes down to is the difference between rough and mean hockey. I would say 90% of the players in the NHL prefer a rough game to one of those free-wheeling, poke-checking affairs. Usually, it's not nearly as rough out there as it looks to the fans. We're well padded and it's noisy when we hit the boards, but as long as we don't stiffen up there isn't too much chance of getting hurt. But hockey gets mean when elbows come into it and guys are working to get your goat or going for you when you haven't got the puck.

Le Petit Diable / 75

When it's rough and legal nobody seems to get mad. You hardly ever see a fight between players who are both clean body checkers. Leo Boivin, who has played with several teams and is one of the toughest and best defensemen in the league, is an example. Boivin could knock you apart with a solid, legal check. Yet I can't recall seeing him in many fights. Bobby Baun seldom got into fights, although he was one of the tougher defensemen. Most of the time he did what he was supposed to legally.

My conversion came early in the 1966–67 season. I guess I had been building up to it for a while. Just as the season started, I noticed that in all the pre-season exhibition games I had only one penalty. And it didn't affect my scoring. I realized I wasn't playing any differently. I was still giving it everything I had—going into the corners, checking and hitting—but legally.

And I finally quit yapping at the referees, although this took more will-power and determination than I knew I had. This sport moves so fast that the officials can't possibly see every infraction, and they make so many split-second decisions that some judgment calls go against you. It's easiest to let off steam with a few appropriate remarks, but you just can't win. There has been much speculation about my "conversion," but the reason for it is really very simple.

When the season began, I got through the first five games without drawing a penalty. I was still scoring and setting up plays, the only difference was that I wasn't spending any time in the penalty box.

I got my first penalty of the season, two minutes for roughing, in the sixth game against Boston in Chicago. It was in the third period and we were leading 3–2. A goal could tie it and there's about twice as good a chance of scoring a goal on a power play, yet here I was resting in the penalty box again.

At that moment, maybe I grew up. I made one of most important decisions of my life: to control my temper, and if I had to retaliate, to do it later, and legally.

From then on, I waited a long time for the chance to get even with a player, maybe while he had his head down and least expected it. Like when I nailed Gordie Howe a couple of seasons ago on Detroit ice.

I couldn't even reach the big lug, let alone hit him. After all, he was three inches taller and about thirty-five pounds heavier.

But he got me roaring mad in Detroit one night when I was coasting into position for a pass in front of their goal. The puck wasn't near me so the officials weren't watching as Howe crossed in front of me. He reefed me with one of those piledriver elbows and I was flat on my back on the ice when the puck came.

It must have been two months later that I got my chance in Chicago. He was circling his own net but having trouble picking up the rolling puck. His head was down—which surprised me—and I caught him squarely with the shoulder on part of his jaw and his chest. It must have hurt because he stared hard at me when he was going off the ice, and I'm sure he knew he was being paid back for something.

My new policy of delayed retaliation also may have been prompted by my daughter, Meg, when she was two years old, near the end of the previous season. She had been watching a Hawks game on TV, when I got a ten-minute misconduct penalty. When I came home, Meg wanted to know how come Daddy spent so much time sitting down while everybody else was skating. It made me stop and think. If a two-year-old could see there was something wrong, why couldn't a twenty-six-year-old find out why he had to be in the penalty box all the time?

I discovered that I didn't have to be. I only had twelve penalty minutes in the 1966–67 season and only fourteen in the 1967–68 season. Both seasons I was awarded the Lady Byng trophy for sportsmanship, but I also was able to lead the league in scoring both seasons, as I had in 1963–64 and 1964–65 when I had been *Le Petit Diable*. They also voted me Most Valuable Player in the league both years. I learned I could play it hard but straight, that a guy could become an expert at handing it out later and mostly within the rules.

Other than the fact that there was no hockey stick long enough to score from the penalty box, there was a background kind of reason for my change. I had the responsibility of providing for my wife and children and paying off the mortgage. If I wanted to build for a future aside from hockey, a guarantee of a good livelihood when my playing days were done, I had to think about my image. A player with a good image can go a lot further. That goes for endorsements and other sources of income while still a player and as a businessman, or in any other field after an athlete's career ends. I don't feel this reason

Le Petit Diable

really influenced me very much, however, because I'm apparently the kind of person who has to be himself no matter what, and I couldn't have done a turnabout just for the sake of image.

It also does something to you to see your youngsters growing up and looking up to you as head of the family. It made me think of the endless stream of kids you run into and how they might make you their hero because your name appears in the papers a lot or because they appreciate your playing. I don't think of myself in terms of being an example for them, because I'm very human with human faults and shortcomings. Yet, all these things had something to do with the conversion of *Le Petit Diable*.

9

Tricks of the Trade

THERE HAVEN'T been many times when I have been so shaken as I was when the Hawks traded Ab McDonald in the summer of 1964. Kenny Wharram telephoned me from North Bay, Ontario, where he spends his summers.

"I just heard we lost our left winger," said Kenny.

"What do you mean?" I asked. I thought Ab had been in an accident.

"Ab has just been traded," Kenny answered.

I don't know whether I asked Kenny to what club or for what players. I just hung up the phone and sat there unable to move. I started thinking . . . why? what were the reasons for the trade? That season Kenny and I each had scored thirty-nine goals and Ab fourteen. That was ninety-two goals, only a few less than the record for a line, and we had the best defensive record of any line in the club, probably the best in the league. We were all plus—that is, had scored a lot more goals than had been scored against us while we were on the ice. I just couldn't believe that there was any good reason to trade Ab. I was really hurt. Besides being a line-mate, Ab had been a good friend, a pal off the ice. Jill tried to talk to me.

"You're a professional," Jill said. "You have to expect this."

Kenny told me the same thing: "You've got to expect to be traded sooner or later. For some it never happens, others get traded four or five times, but in any case every hockey player has to realize that it can happen to him at any time."

I tried to think along those lines but I was still bitter at the management. I couldn't understand the reason for making the trade. It was said the club needed defensive help and more scoring punch on the left side of our line. Ab and Reggie Fleming had been traded to Boston for defenseman Doug Mohns, and they counted on one of the kids they were bringing up the next season to play left wing on our line. But I thought, "If you get ninety-two goals out of one line, that should be enough. What more can you expect?" I think more than anything else I was hurt because of my friendship with Ab. As it turned out, when Mohns became our left wing he did a terrific job, too. But Ab's leaving hurt me personally. I'm sure Bobby Hull and Chico Maki felt the same way four years later when the Hawks traded Phil Esposito, not only because they had lost a fine center but because of friendship.

Every athlete has a feeling that sooner or later in his career he is going to be traded, but it always seems to come when he least expects it, and it's a great shock. I know I had that feeling all during the 1968–69 season, thinking constantly that there might be something brewing. At that time, nothing happened. But you can't help thinking about it because of all the changes it could make in your life. It's not so much that I've settled down in Chicago, because after all most of the players in the league live in cities other than the ones in which they play. It would be nothing unusual for me to play for, say, Toronto and live in Chicago. It just happens to be more convenient to live in the same city as the one in which you play your hockey. Still, the shock of being traded would be great. I've formed a lot of friendships in Chicago and while I'm sure I would find new friends elsewhere, I treasure the ones I have.

The shock probably would be greater for my wife. Since we've been married we've never had to move as so many other hockey families do at the beginning and end of each season. And she was born and raised in the Chicago area, but she has said she could live with it and knows she would have to if it ever happened because I earn my livelihood in hockey.

I've also heard of players who have been shocked into improvement by being traded. It can happen once in a while that a man gets complacent in one town and the shock of being traded needles him to life. Still, trades are hard on friendships.

Naturally the next thing you're most concerned about is what is going to happen out on the ice, who's going to pick up the slack. Are you going to find another player who will fit in with you the same way? After all, you can have the greatest hockey player in the world on your line but if you can't play with him there's no sense in his being there. If you have the right line-mates you understand each other both on and off the ice. You can talk to each other. If one of them is carrying the puck down the ice, you know his moves, you anticipate what he's going to do, and you try to get in a spot where you'll end up in one place because you know he's going to end up in the other. You can achieve this cooperation and teamwork with only certain guys. With others, it might take years to develop, and even then you might never fit in smoothly.

I kept worrying about that in training camp during the fall of 1964. Coach Reay put us with John Brenneman, Doug Robinson, and some other kids who were pretty good hockey players, but they didn't seem to fit in with our style of play. We went this way through the early season, and things weren't going too well.

I don't know whether it was Kenny or I who first thought of getting Doug Mohns on our line, but I remember looking at Mohnsie coming out of the end zone with the puck looking like a big diesel engine ("Dougie, the Diesel," we called him) without anybody being able to touch him. Kenny and I thought, "If we just had that guy playing left wing with us." In a way, Mohnsie moved the puck out something like Ab did. He'd get the puck in a corner and you couldn't take it away from him. His style of skating and carrying the puck was a little different from Ab's, but they both could get the job done, which is what we were looking for. One day we casually mentioned to Reay that it might be worth trying Mohnsie with us. He gave the impression he thought we were crazy but after a while he decided to try it and we clicked. I have a hunch Billy was thinking of the move anyway.

It's strange. You can just take a look at one person and say, "I think I could play with that guy," and you could look at somebody else and say, "No, I don't think I could play with him." The tip-offs are the way he handles the puck and the way he passes, because our line throws the puck around quite a bit and if the pass isn't perfect we don't just keep on skating. We stop, pick up the puck, make sure we control it. We chase it whether it's behind us or in front of us. If we have to dive for it, we do. That's the way the Scooter Line always has been.

With Mohnsie, we could use the same plays we had been using with Ab, and we could talk them over and develop them the same way. Mohnsie is different off the ice from Ab, but just as likeable. He's quiet and doesn't like to go out as much for lunch or beers after practice or on the road. But he came along. If we had four beers, he'd have two. If we had two, he'd have one.

Tricks of the Trade / 81

With Ab gone, it no longer was one man leading the line, it was three leading each other. Kenny and I might say, "Doug, this is the way we've always done it," and he'd say, "Fine, let's try it," but then he might come up with an idea. He contributed just as much in this way as Kenny and I did.

The Scooter Line with Mohnise was just as successful as it had been with Ab. We started playing together part way through the 1964-65 season and the next four seasons each of us scored twenty or more goals every year. You can go up and down the league and you won't find a line that did that four years in a row. We were able to do it because we worked together perfectly and because we forced the play. We weren't a checking line just trying to keep the opposition from scoring, but a forcing line. We made the plays and let the opposition worry about checking us; we kept them busy so they couldn't score.

The funny thing is that people thought we were magicians or something, when all we really did was make the obvious plays. Most of the time we didn't do anything unusual or surprising. We just kept skating and each of us sensed where the other would be. We didn't have to do a lot of yelling on the ice. The only time we yelled was if we were really open. If it looked like only a fifty-fifty chance of being open for a pass, we didn't yell. But if it was 75 to 100% that we were open and would be able to get the puck if it was close to us, we yelled either "Whip" for Kenny, "Mohnsie" or "Kita."

I give Ab, Kenny and Mohnsie a lot of the credit for the four scoring titles I won. It's the man in the open that makes the scoring play, and they were there more often than not. That's how you pile up assists. I know what I owe them.

But I was also a different player by this time than I had been as a kid. I had learned a good deal about what I could and couldn't do and about how I had to play against certain men, particularly such fine centers as Norm Ullman, Jean Beliveau, Dave Keon, and Henri Richard and goaltenders such a Gump Worsley, Eddie Giacomin and Johnny Bower.

Over the years, Ullman, first with Detroit and then with Toronto, has been the toughest man for me to play against. Keon of Toronto has been second. Ullman never stopped dogging or checking me. When the puck was shot in our end and I'd go back and pick it up, although I might have two full strides on him, he'd be suddenly moving just as fast as I was or even a little faster. Ullman always had that stick around me somewhere, either pulling at me, hooking or using his favorite, the sweep-check from behind. He knew exactly what he was doing with the stick and he could take the puck away from me at least 90% of the time unless I got my body in front of him, but that slowed me down so somebody else could get me. He also was great at lateral skating as when two defensemen passed the puck back and forth between them. We had different styles. His was stopping and starting a good bit, mine was always keeping in motion, turning.

Keon played similarly except that he was a little smaller and he could skate faster in a straight line. Normie looked like he was laboring on skates, making more of an effort than Keon.

I adjusted in one respect to both of them. They didn't play my body too much when they reached from behind. They played the puck, so I learned to move it a little more quickly. In other words, I held it a split second longer with somebody else checking me, but if it were Ullman or Keon I'd pass it off a little faster. Naturally, they were hoping to hurry me because in that case the pass wasn't going to be as accurate.

You adjust your style against certain goaltenders, too, although shooting at the net is largely a case of what the situation is at the time. If you've got a screen shot, you just let it go fast and hope you hit the corner of the net. If you've got a breakaway, your move depends on the goalie's. If he comes out to block the angle, you have to try to deke him. If he starts to back up on you, then you have to make up your mind whether to keep deking him or shoot the puck.

When Worsley was with New York he was a sort of fall-down goaltender. He would fall down making the stop and didn't recover quickly to be ready for the rebound. Later with Montreal he became more of a stand-up goaltender and played the angles more. He often gave you a big opening to shoot at, expecting you to try and sneak one past, but he'd be ready for it.

You have to try and deke more on a stand-up goalie than one who falls down. And you have to shoot quickly on a fall-down goalie because when he's falling he'll have everything going for him, stick, foot, arm, and even head.

When it came to face-offs, Phil Goyette of New York was the toughest for me to beat, although Beliveau took a draw beautifully and both Ullman and Keon were good. You have been on my head. The young Hawk wearing number 3 is Pierre Pilote, Glen Hall is in goal and Eric Nesterenko is in the background.

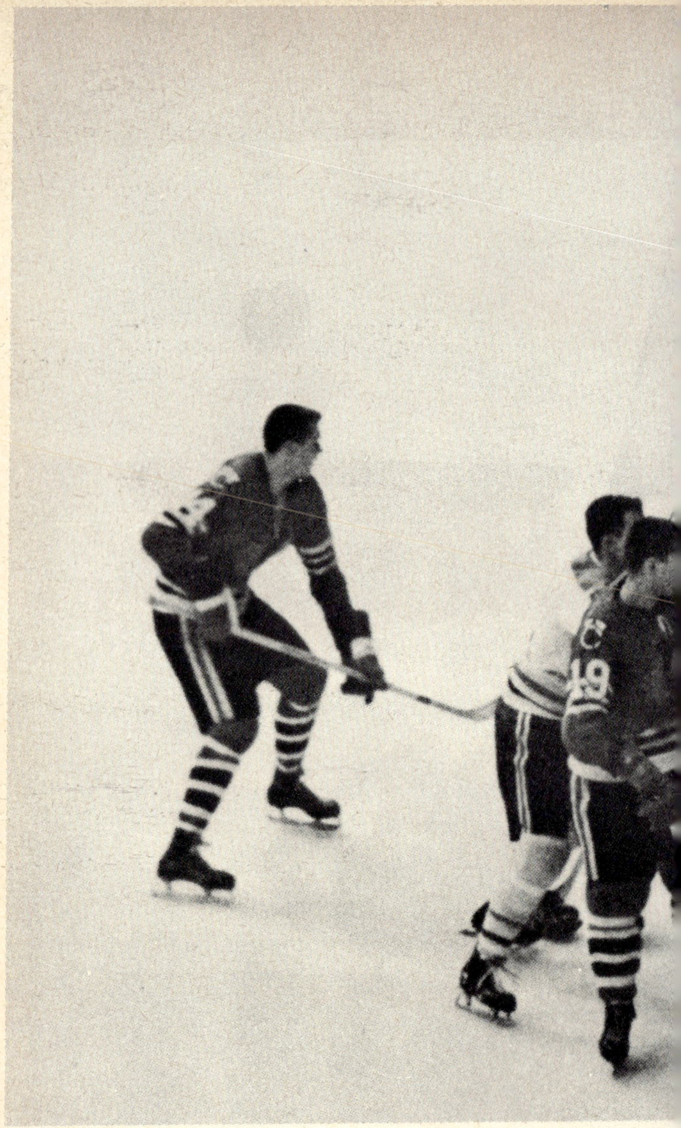

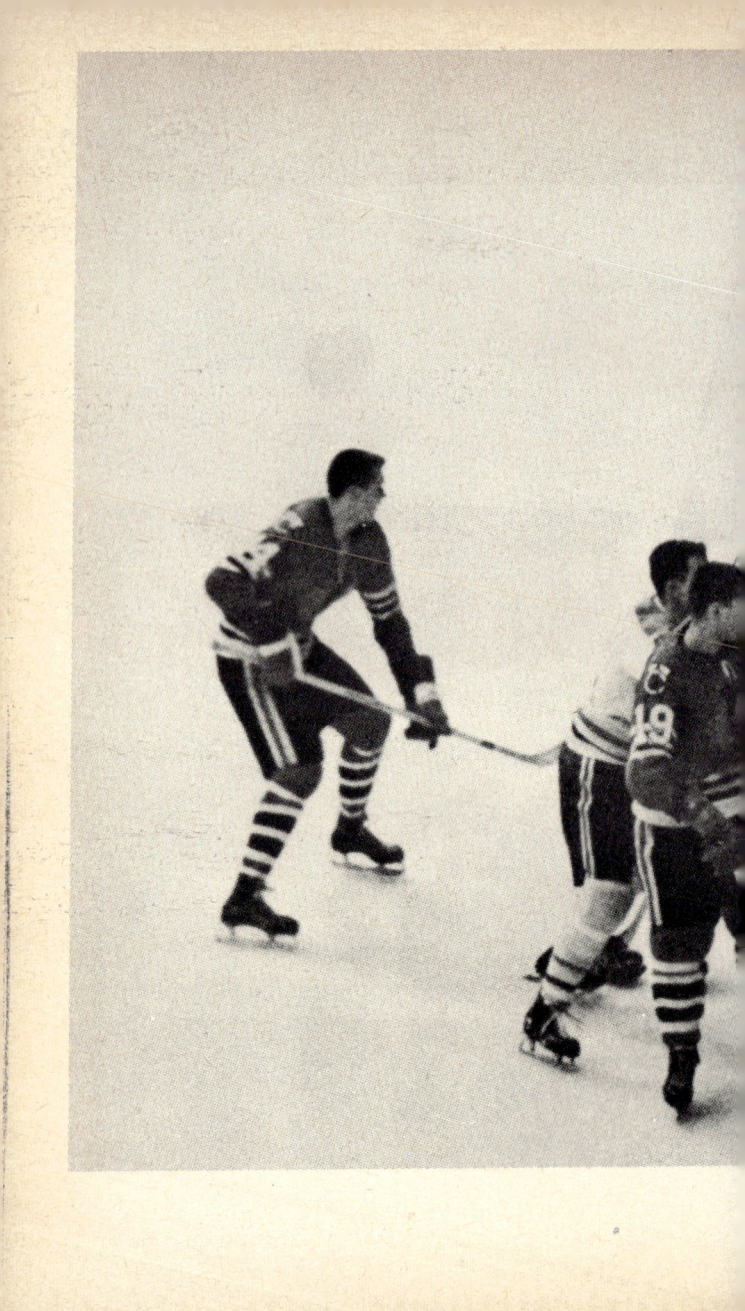

Henri Richard and I tangled a few times before I got smart enough to avoid these silly penalties. This was in Chicago in 1961, and of course Henri is number 16.

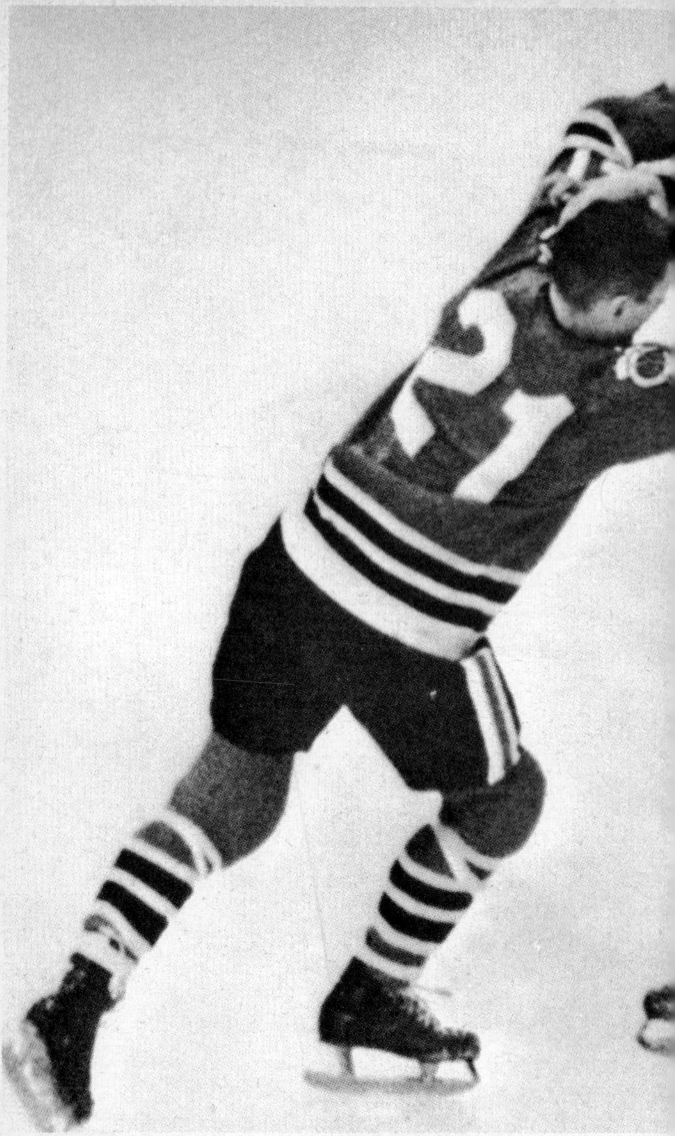

Tom Johnson was a friend of mine off the ice but you'd never know it from this 1964 photograph, taken in Chicago. Neither of us was kidding.

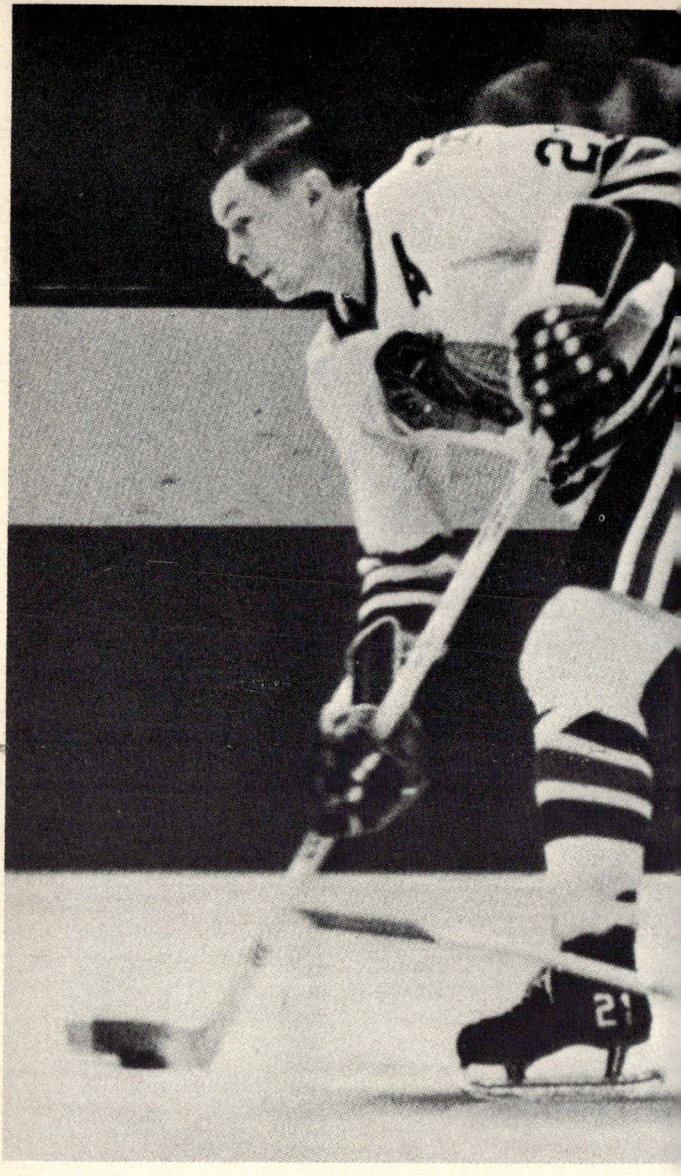

A fast slap shot should mean a goal. I can't remember whether this one did or not.

Here I'm facing off against Tom Johnson of the New York Rangers.

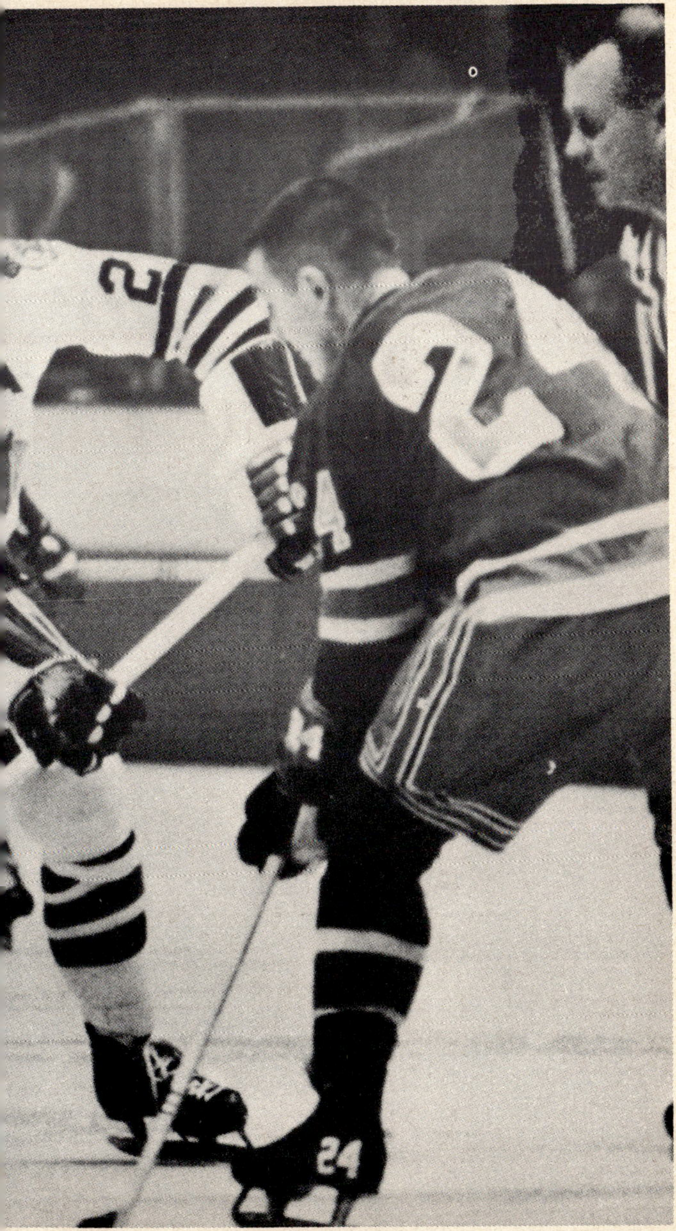
24

In January 1966 we were in action against the New York Rangers. Bill Hicke and Doug Jarrett are in the background.

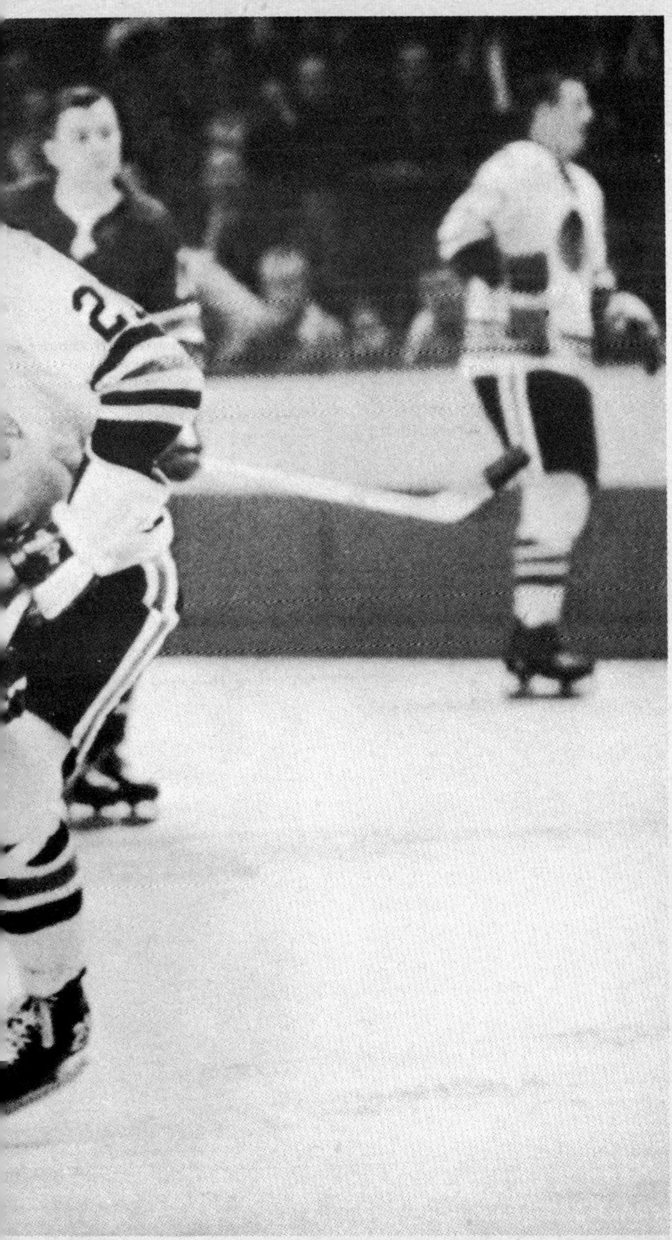

Despite anything my old buddies may think, I was shooting the puck past Larry Hillman, not trying to remove his kneecap.

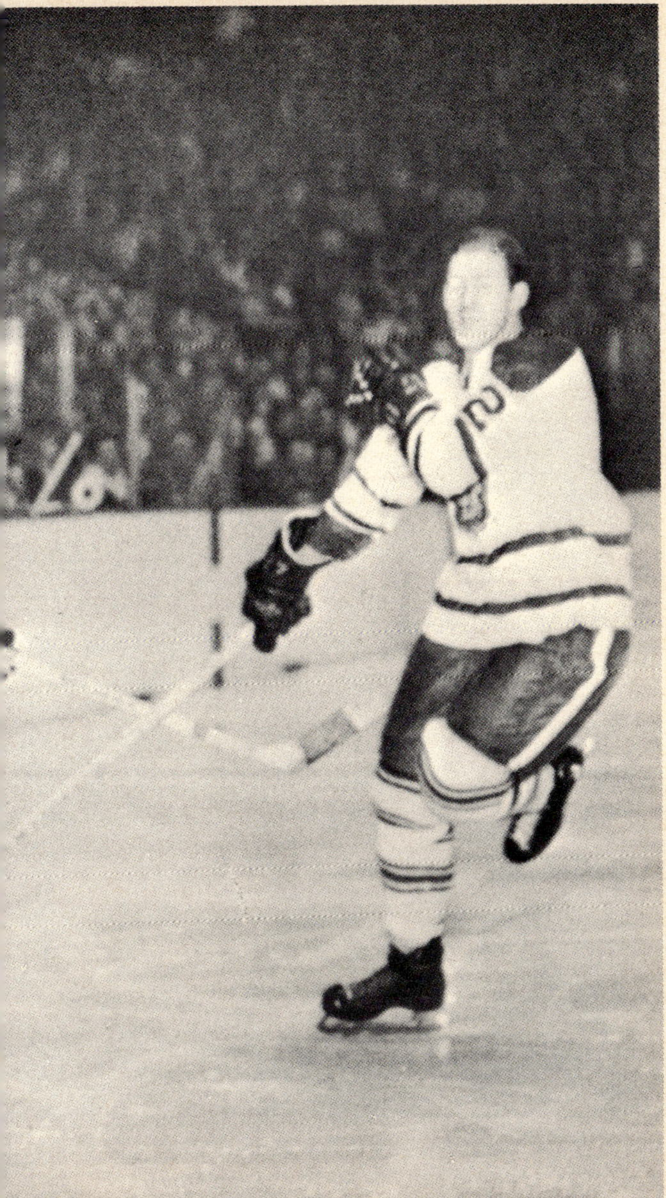

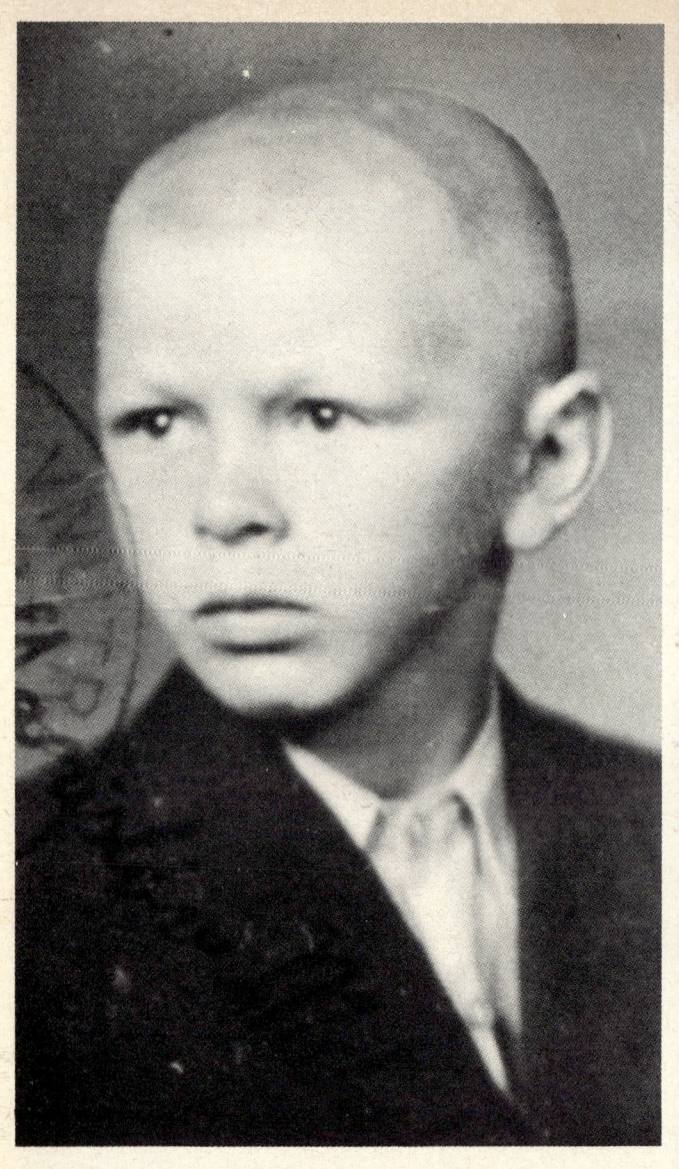

As an eight-year-old, in 1948 I came to Canada, and this is what I looked like. Puzzled, maybe; apprehensive, certainly, but really not afraid.

On arrival in Czechoslovakia, a returning native son is greeted with a ceremony involving bread and salt. I bit into the bread but forgot about the teeth I'd lost in the hockey wars.

On our trip abroad Jill still seems game but Meg—like any little girl—is tired enough to need carrying. This was taken in Kosice.

This is Czechoslovakia in 1967. Joe Golonka, captain of the Czech National team, is leaning against the boards. His team certainly knew what they were about.

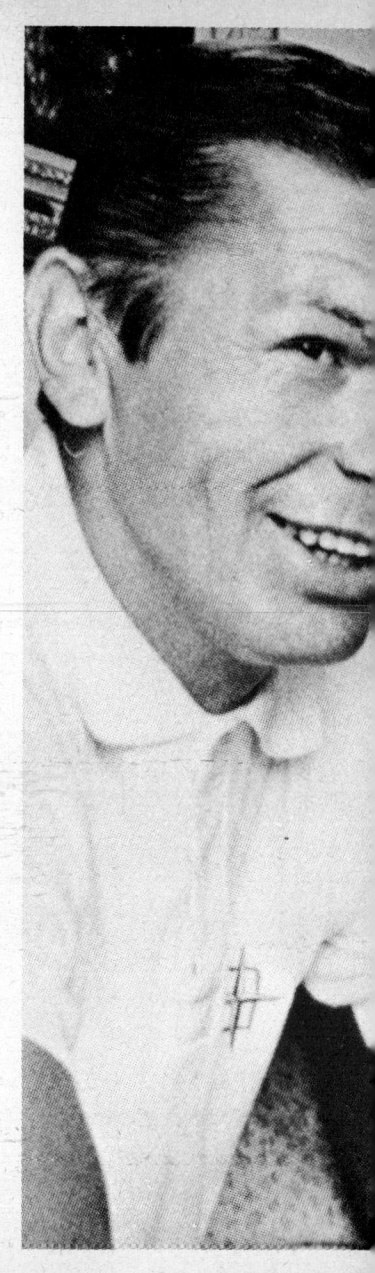

In 1968 my sister Viera and my real mother visited us at my home in Elmhurst. It's not hard to tell how glad I was to see them both.

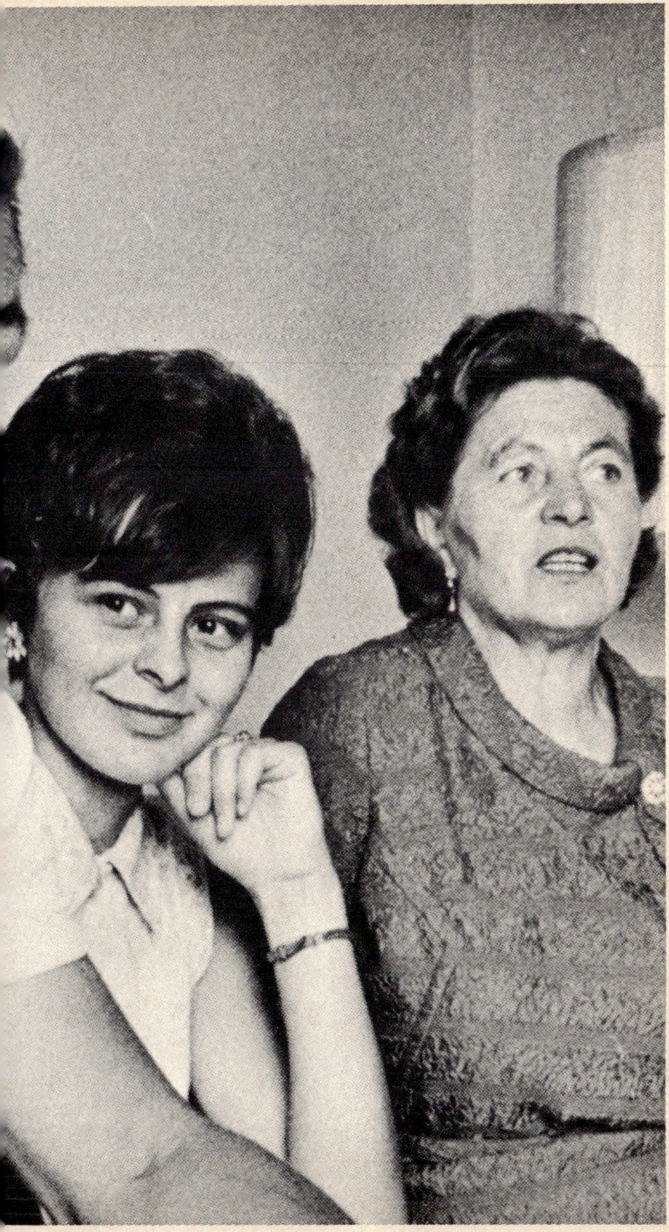

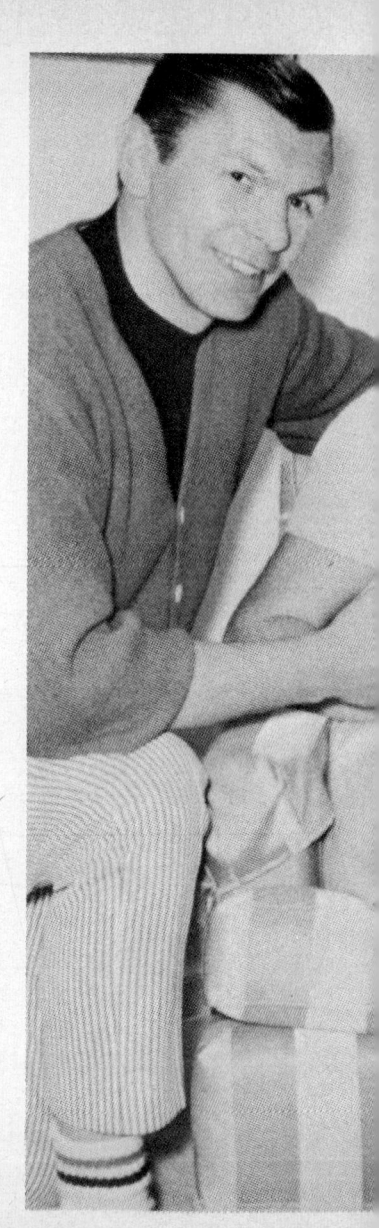

What a gang! All wonderful, but a handful just the same. Jane is on her mother's lap and Meg is sitting next to her. Scott is the young man on the right.

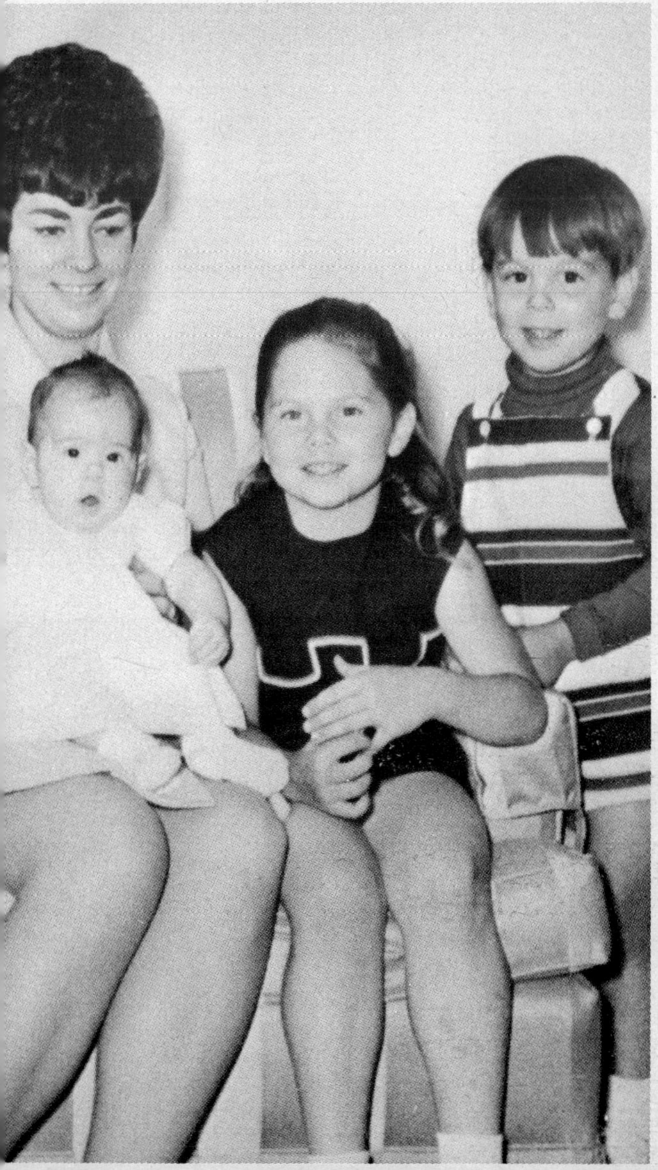

This is a pretty good action shot of a game against the New York Rangers. That's Matt Ravelich behind me, and it looks as though I was trying to block Vic Hadfield's shot.

Tricks of the Trade / 83

to be mentally right before you step into the face-off circle. You can't be thinking of anything but winning the draw, making sure you get the puck to one of your teammates, because if you get beaten, especially in your own end of the ice, it can be tough. A lost draw can quickly lead to a goal for the other team.

It helps to know your opponent when facing off. Most players will use their backhand. Once in a while, to cross you up, they'll go the other way, forward or even backward on the forehand. You look to see which way the other is positioned. If he's leaning toward you, you know he's going forward with the puck. If he's leaning back, you know what he has in mind. You can't tell all the time, because some are good at hiding their intentions, but if they give themselves away a little it helps. I concentrate on the face-off because often it can mean the difference between winning and losing a game. I think that over the years I improved my ability to get the draw.

I know my shot improved, or at least that I developed my speed in getting it off, and my accuracy. When I was a junior we'd have a board in the center of the net with the four corners open so that we'd shoot at those. When I came up to the Hawks, I'd practice shooting at the posts. I knew if I could get my shot down fine enough to hit the posts I could put it in the net when I had to. I'd also shoot at the blue and red lines running up the boards at the blue and red lines on the ice. You know if you can come close to hitting those from center ice you're fairly accurate from twenty to thirty feet away from the net.

At first I mostly used the wrist shot. I didn't really know how to slap the puck well in a hurry. I had to work on getting the slap shot away quickly, and I never had what you'd call an overpowering one. When Bobby Hull shot, it was both quick and heavy. The difference between a heavy shot and a fast shot is the force with which it reaches the goalie. He can catch the fast shot in his glove and while it may knock back the webbing it won't jolt his wrist. A heavy shot will hit the glove and not only knock back the webbing but take the goalie's arm with it. It's like the difference between one pitcher's fast ball and another's. Some just throw a baseball fast, others throw it hard. The same with a puck. I think it has something to do with the timing and the speed with which the sticks meets the puck.

Once you master the slap shot and have a little time to get it away, you know you're going to get off a pretty good shot. By the same token, you can't wait so long that you start thinking about where to put it instead of just slapping the puck. It's like a putt in golf. If you stand over it too long you're sure to mess it up one way or the other because your muscles are going to tighten. With a puck, if you've got too much time to think, you end up shooting it right at the goalie. I worked on the slapshot three or four years, after which I was able to score a few goals from the blue line.

There are several ways of shooting the wrist shot. There are some experts like Alex Delvecchio of Detroit who snap it away, using wrist and forearm muscles. His is an all-arms shot. Mine is also a body shot, I have to use my legs with it. Normally, I keep the weight on one leg and it doesn't matter really which one it is although according to some people you should keep the weight on the leg opposite the side you're shooting from. I'm a right-hand shot so I keep my weight on my left leg and keep my right leg out of the way so I won't hit it with the stick when sweeping the puck forward. I've tried to use Delvecchio's way of snapping the puck, but with little success.

When I came into the NHL I had a good backhand shot. At the time I was using a straight stick, and after shooting the puck that way for a number of years you should be able to get off a good backhander or you've got no business being in the game. But when I changed to the curved stick, I had to learn the backhand shot all over again.

I discovered the curved stick almost by accident during practice in March 1961, my second season with the Hawks. For a time, trying to develop the stick and learning how to use it created almost as many problems for me as the stick did for goalies later when it was used by Bobby Hull, who was quick to take it up. More about that later. The point here is that whether it's switching to a curved stick, developing a new twist to a play, adjusting to the guys you play with and against, or any other aspect of the game, you can't stand still, you have to keep looking for new ways to do things on the ice. If you don't, there'll be no need to look back to see if somebody's gaining on you—he'll be ahead of you.

10

Champions

SOME EXPERTS say the Black Hawks choked, faded, or folded year after year, but I refuse to think of it that way. Sure, a lot of years we led the league going into the stretch only to drop into second or third place at the end, and many of the fans and press were quick to call us "choke-up artists." I didn't like these statements and don't think they're true.

The fact is that we didn't win enough games because we just weren't good enough, or didn't have depth on the bench to take up the slack due to injuries or regulars getting tired.

What made it tough was that people seemed sure we had the best team in the league during the five years after we won the Stanley Cup in 1960–61. After all, we had the league's top goal-scorer in Bobby Hull, its finest goalie in Glenn Hall, the outstanding defenseman in Pierre Pilote, and our Scooter Line was going strong. In 1963–64, five of us were selected to the NHL All-Star first team: Hall, Pilote, Hull, Wharram, and myself, and defenseman Moose Vasko made the second team. People looked at that and thought, "Holy cow! How can a team like that miss finishing first?"

Every March it was the same thing. With the championship in sight, we went into a slump or slowed down and either Montreal, Toronto or Detroit would pass us to take the Prince of Wales Trophy. People even began wondering if there really wasn't something to Muldoon's Curse, a jinx that supposedly had kept the Hawks from finishing first ever since they entered the league in 1926. The curse allegedly was made by the team's first coach, Pete Muldoon, when he was fired in 1927.

I had never heard of Muldoon's Curse until we had one of our best shots at first place but ended up second. I didn't know who Muldoon was and couldn't have cared less. It had nothing to do with me. I went out there and gave the best every time, but sometimes my best wasn't good enough and the same could be said of the rest of the team.

What it really came down to was that until 1966–67 we didn't have the bench strength and overall balance and we haven't since. We didn't have anybody to step in and give us a lift when the regulars wore down. As the season goes along you tire out and lose weight, and the game itself starts to get to you. You can become sick and tired of it by the time the playoffs roll around. You just can't psych yourself into getting keyed up for every one of seventy or seventy-six games. You try to do it for as many as possible; but as the season nears its end, you can't help at times thinking about something else and that's when you need a little more rest and somebody fresh to pick up the team.

We got just the kind of players we needed in 1966–67, in defenseman Ed Van Impe and forwards Lou Angotti, Dennis Hull, Wally Boyer and Ken Hodge. When you start putting fresh faces into a lineup, the others' momentum picks up and they start hustling to keep up and avoid being put on the bench or shipped out.

Van Impe, Dennis Hull, and Angotti weren't completely new to us. We had added Angotti during the 1965–66 season and Van Impe and Dennis Hull had been to training camp in previous years. In fact, Dennis had spent most of the 1964–65 season with the Hawks, being farmed out the next year.

Van Impe was a big tough guy who could clear opposing players from in front of our net, drive them into the corners, or stop them at the blue line with body checks. He was just what we needed and had a great season, teamed up with Pat Stapleton, who played the game something like Pilote did, handling the puck well and thinking all the time. Stapleton didn't hit too often but he was two moves ahead of everybody else as a great anticipator of plays.

Our other defensive pair, Dougie Jarrett and Pilote, also had a great year. Jarrett was a strong hitter, and Pierre hit a man once in a while, but he wouldn't run after him. When Pilote hit a man you knew he had him lined up and the player was either off balance or had his head down. Pierre was great with the puck coming out of our end. You knew when he got hold of it he was sure to get it out of there. Matt Ravlich was the fifth defenseman and he fit in well whenever he was needed.

Let's face it, we had a pretty good team in 1966–67. You

could go up and down that lineup and you couldn't find a weak spot. Glenn Hall and Dennis DeJordy gave us the best goaltending in the league and won the Vezina Trophy. We had a lot of speed, men like Wharram, Mohns, Bobby Hull, and Chico Maki could fly up front and we had forwards that could hit, too. Mohns was stepping into the opposition, Bobby was running right over them, and Phil Esposito, who centered for Bobby and Chico, was hitting the odd man here and there. We weren't exerted too much at the halfway point of the season because we had a balanced club with all three lines scoring. When Bill Hay rejoined us at mid-season to center for Eric Nesterenko on the right and Dennis Hull at left wing, we had as good a defensive line as you could expect, but one that could score, too. And Nesterenko and Hay were the best penalty killers around.

We had a strong bench. You could have thrown anybody out on the ice and get the job done. We were lucky, too. We didn't have three or four injuries to key men at any one time, and when somebody was hurt we had the men to step in and play without slowing us up. Let's say Wharram was hurt, Angotti was ready to go on right wing. If Mohns was hurt, Angotti could play left wing. If I were injured, Angotti was in there at center. There was a man who could play anywhere and you knew he'd not only do a good job but pick up the whole team with his spirit. Boyer and Hodge were just as willing, and Kenny could throw his weight around a little.

I'm convinced that training camp can make or break your season. It means a lot to me, and I went into it in the fall of 1966 with the determination to work harder than ever, hoping this would rub off on some of the others. I think every player has somebody he looks up to and if he sees that man working he's going to work a little harder, too. That's the way I felt about it and it might have had a little bearing on the other fellows. We all worked hard in camp and in practice all season, and if you work hard in those two things you'll work hard in games.

We couldn't have had a better start to a season, Bobby and I scoring two goals apiece in the opener to beat New York 6–3 and get off to a four-game winning streak. We lost just two of the first twelve games and DeJordy did a fine job of goaltending until Hall ended his holdout, or finished painting his barn, and came back to start the sixth game.

We had a fine record of eighteen won, ten lost, and five tied, but were still in a tight battle with New York for first place when Tommy Ivan made the move that eventually guaranteed us our first Prince of Wales Trophy. Ivan got Bill Hay, who had retired after the 1965–66 season, to rejoin us on January 11, 1967. We beat Detroit 6–1 that night, with Bobby Hull getting three goals; lost the next game, then went off on a fifteen-game unbeaten streak, winning twelve and tying three, to move fourteen points in front of the league.

Hay was a natural born leader. I know I had a lot of respect for him. Besides being a terrific two-way hockey player, he could lead off the ice as well as on it, and he kept the team together. If we were on the road, say in Montreal, he'd get Pilote, the captain, to tell us: "Okay, we're all going out together after the game. Everybody shows up tonight at the Green Door and we'll have some beers and talk hockey."

It's hard to explain how much that meant to us. We'd sit there, drink beer, and talk about the mistakes we'd made, how we could avoid them in the future, and about anything else that had to be brought out in the open. Maybe we'd criticize each other. There are some players who can't stand criticism, but why should that be? We were pros, not amateurs. If I'm doing something wrong on the ice, I want to know about it. Don't tell me my good points, tell me the bad ones. That's how you help each other and that's what we did at these meetings.

Hay had the knack of controlling people. He never said too much but when he did open his mouth you knew that whatever came out would be common sense and would be worth taking in. He also had a dry sense of humor and once in a while said something that went over a few heads because it had a double meaning. But Hay contributed as much to our winning the championship off the ice as he did on it, which was plenty.

Hay was a remarkable man in many ways. He didn't really need the money he got from hockey as he came from a comparatively wealthy family. Bill's father was president of the British American Oil Company. After his high school education Bill went on to Colorado College, in Denver, and took a degree in geology. He followed this career during the off-season and is now a successful geologist working out of Calgary, Alberta. Bill won the Calder Cup in 1959–60 when he was chosen the rookie of the year. He broke his retirement after the 1965–66 season only because the Hawks' management told him they needed him to win the championship. At their urging he returned for the half season with only one thing in mind, to help the Hawks to that first Prince of Wales Cup.

Not that we were sure we had it won even after the streak which carried us into mid-February. We remembered only too well the previous seasons, when we had stopped winning at the end. We saw stories in the newspapers with headlines like, "Can Hawks Avoid Fade in Stretch?" The more you read about it, the more you started thinking about it. You tried to avoid it, but the more you try in hockey, the more likely you are to sort of tighten up, to stop playing your natural game, and then you're really in trouble.

There was a moment's doubt when we lost 3–0 at Toronto on March 4, but we beat them the next day 5–2, beat Boston 3–1, and tied Montreal 3–3, after being down 3–0 at one point of the game. We showed that we could bounce back as we had all season, and on March 12 we played Toronto at the Chicago stadium in a Sunday afternoon game that could clinch the championship for us.

I know that we all were a little more tense for that game than we had been previously. Normally, when the team is keyed up it shows in either one of two ways. You can all sit there like a bunch of college kids giving it the "Rah, rah, let's go, boys," or sit there and not say a word, saving your energy and spirit for the game. That afternoon nobody said much before the game. I get nervous before every game, but that particular one I was more keyed up than ever. Everyone seemed to feel the same way.

Not on the ice, though. I can tell almost from the first shift how a game is going to go. The way we started out, skating like hell, I knew we weren't going to lose—we'd either tie it or win it. I used to think that if a player felt good in the warm-up, he'd feel good in the game. Actually, it worked in reverse for me. If I felt bad in the warm-up, I usually felt good in the game, and it was like that in the Toronto game. I didn't have to work at the skating, it came like a fluid, paced type of thing. Not that I scored a goal. If I was in good position to shoot, I'd take a shot, but the puck would flip on me, jump over my stick, hit a goal post, or hit somebody on the ankle. But everybody was skating that day and, as it had been doing all season, the bench gave us the lift we needed for a victory. Kenny Hodge and Angotti each got a pair of goals, with Bobby Hull getting the other one.

The first goal came midway in the opening period, with Esposito passing the puck out from the left corner to Hodge near the right post, and he batted it past Toronto goalie Terry Sawchuk. Hodge got another one four minutes later when Esposito centered from the right face-off circle to where Hodge and Bobby Hull were fighting to stay in front of the net. Bobby got a skate on the puck and kicked it over to Hodge, who knocked it into the net. Hodge wasn't through for the period. He assisted on the third goal, one of Bobby's backhanders.

We knew we had that game after the third goal, particularly with Glenn Hall in our net. Angotti's two in the third period were just frosting on the cake and we could hardly wait for the game to end so we could break into the champagne. That 5–0 victory put Muldoon's Curse to rest and, more important, no one could accuse us any longer of "choking up." Or so we thought at the time.

I've seen films of the celebration in our dressing room after the game, and it was a wild scene with the champagne bubbling down throats, over shirts and hair, and squirting in all directions. I remember we carried Ivan and Reay into the shower stalls and pushed them fully dressed under the nozzles. It's hard to imagine a bunch of grown men acting like kids, but we couldn't have been happier and, in a situation like that, you can't really control your emotions. Relief, joy, whatever it is, makes you do the craziest things and add to the sweetness of having achieved a goal you've been reaching for year after year without success. All our efforts were aimed at finishing first that season, maybe partly to wipe out the memory of the years in which we had just missed making it.

We didn't let down consciously after clinching the title. In fact, we lost only three of the remaining nine games, winning four and tying two, which was pretty fair for a team having nothing more at stake until the playoffs. Our record of 41 won, 17 lost, and 12 tied was the best in Black Hawk history, and we set a league record with 264 goals scored. Bobby had 52 goals, just two less than his record total of the previous season, and I had 97 points on 35 goals and 62 assists. The 97 points matched the league record set by Bobby the year before and the 62 assists were a new high.

Champions / 91

I'd be insincere if I didn't admit that winning the Hart Trophy as the league's most valuable player, the Ross Trophy as leading scorer, and the Lady Byng trophy for sportsmanship was a great personal satisfaction, especially since nobody had ever won all three in one season in the entire fifty-year history of the league. Still, what really made it satisfying was that it was done as a contribution to a winning team.

The trouble is that we were winners only up to a point. Looking back, it's clear that we had reached a certain physical and mental peak in the 5-0 victory over Toronto that clinched first place. We had nothing else to shoot for in the regular season and we subconsciously let down. We couldn't really get up mentally for the rest of the games, and we may have worried about getting hurt and worn out for the playoffs. But when you let up a little bit, it's tough to regain the right mental attitude, and that's what determines winners in a short series. Maybe part of the reason that we lost the playoffs was that we were too satisfied with the championship, that we weren't hungry enough for the Stanley Cup even though we had a great team. Toronto seemed to have more fire, and acted hungrier. We had lost our edge, we weren't sharp.

Just as in 1960-61 when we had won the triple overtime game over Montreal to take the big step toward the Stanley Cup, the turning point in the semifinal series with Toronto in 1966-67 came long before the end. It came in the second game, played Sunday, April 9, in Chicago, after we had taken an edge by winning the opening game the previous Thursday. With Terry Sawchuk stopping almost everything we threw at him, the underdog Leafs won the second game 3-1 on our ice. We played pretty well, but we just couldn't put enough pucks in the net. The victory had the same effect on Toronto as our victory did for us against Montreal six years before. It gave them the lift they needed, and they took the series in six games, then went on to beat Montreal in the finals.

Really, it's a matter of the letdown hurting the losing club more than the upsurge helps the winners in a game like our 3-1 loss to Toronto. They know they can win by playing the same way, while you feel you've put out all the effort you could and still have nothing to show for it. Whatever the reason, you've lost the game, and you can give a logical explanation but you can't control your mind and emotions. The winning team gets a mental edge, and the team that is mentally and emotionally better off will wind up the series winner.

We lost the sixth game and the semifinals in Toronto. When we landed in Chicago, I knew there would be a crowd waiting for us at the airport so I grabbed the intercom on the plane and told the fellows: "Let's walk off this plane with our heads up. We have nothing to be ashamed of. We played our best, it just wasn't good enough." I wasn't much for making speeches but I just felt like saying it because the team members had their heads down and I wanted them to get off that plane feeling proud of what they had accomplished that season. Also, it was no way to part. We weren't going to see each other until fall and, as it turned out, a lot of us didn't see each other in the same uniforms again.

Quite a bit of the joy of the season and that first-place finish was gone for me by losing in the playoffs, and I felt deeply disappointed. Many of the fans and newspapermen didn't help. I guess it's human nature for people to forget very quickly what you've accomplished and to harp on your failures. A large percentage of fans in any sport are front-runners; when you're winning they're with you, if you're losing you're a bum.

After the playoffs, if somebody recognized me on the street one of two things would happen:

"Congratulations on winning the championship," a few would say.

"What the hell happened to you in the playoffs?" others would ask, and they added up to 90%.

Most people looked only at the bad side instead of considering the good side, too. I started feeling the same way until Billy Reay came up to me and said, "Don't feel disappointed about the Stanley Cup. We got one thing and maybe next year we'll get both."

He was right! Life's too tough and too short to worry about the disappointments, so why not think about and enjoy the good things and go out to overcome the others.

11

Bobby and I

MOSTLY I JUST laugh it off, but there are times when I get sick of all the stories about how Bobby Hull and Stan Mikita are feuding, or that Mikita is jealous because Hull gets more attention.

Most of the people who bring up these same things over and over again are newspaper and magazine writers who may be hard up for a story. I guess they figure that nothing pleases editors and attracts readers more than stories of controversy, so they write that Mikita and Hull aren't talking to each other and the team is suffering.

And scarcely a week goes by without writers making comparisons and talking about who's No. 1 and who's No. 2. I'll admit it's nice to read or hear it when somebody says you're better than somebody else, although it depends a lot on who it's coming from. If it's somebody knowledgeable about the game, you especially appreciate it. But you ignore it when it comes from someone trying to flatter you, and you laugh it off when it comes from the opposition. There have been times when the opposition tries to goad you into making a statement that would start something. Toronto has tried it a couple of times. Punch Imlach, who coached Toronto, or King Clancy, his assistant, or the newspapermen have said, "Mikita's the guy that makes the team go, and when he's going the Hawks are going," or "Hull's the guy that gets the team going." They hoped to get Bobby mad at me or the other way around. I don't like this kind of thing and neither does Bobby, so we laugh and forget it.

They're right in only one way: Bobby and I compete with each other, but it's friendly competition, the kind that benefits the team because we both go out on the ice trying to do our best, and if one of us happens to lead the league in scoring it certainly doesn't hurt the Hawks to have the other one come in second.

Bobby and I have been friends for a long time. When I first came to Chicago and walked into the dressing room he came over and put his arm around me. He made me feel at home, and we roomed together for a year and half. We ran around together, we double-dated, we went to shows. We were good friends then and we're good friends now, and people writing or saying that Bobby Hull is No. 1 doesn't change that. It's fine with me, I've always said that, too, and when somebody approaches Bobby, he says Stan is No. 1. It really makes no difference. I've always tried to do my best and set my sights to become No. 1, and whether I am or not, I don't know. In my own head and heart, I know I try my darndest and don't think of myself as No. 2.

Frequently, these stories say that Mikita is jealous of all the publicity Bobby is getting, and that if Mikita got more, he'd make more money because he'd be more in demand for commercials and endorsements. Well, I've gotten my share of ink, and I just can't expect to get the kind of publicity Bobby does.

A long time ago, I looked into a mirror and realized I wasn't the best-looking guy in the world. I don't have blond hair like Bobby and nobody called me the Golden Jet or the Blond Bomber. I didn't get a nickname or the glamor build-up in the way that Bobby got it. I don't have the natural good looks that Bobby has, but then he's got a few scars, too. But the fact is that he looks a lot better in a swimsuit than I do.

Then there are the differences in our public personalities and in our styles of playing the game.

Bobby can be nice anytime he wants to be. I had to work at it. I couldn't really be nice to anybody, not even my wife, when we just had blown a game we should have won or somebody creamed us by four or five goals. It wasn't in my character, in my makeup. Writers made an issue of that, saying Mikita is a surly so-and-so while Hull is the All-American kid next door who shows his pearly white teeth every chance he gets, and nobody ever sees him with a frown on his face. Well, that's the way he is, and I'm the way I am.

One reason people have given Bobby this good guy image is because he does stop, does sign autographs, no matter where he is, whether we win, lose or draw, on the road or at home. Even if we have just a few minutes to catch a bus, train or

Bobby and I / 95

plane, he'll never leave even five kids standing there without making sure they get his autograph, and he can cut the schedule pretty close. I get too uncomfortable if I keep others waiting. But as long as it makes some kids happy, Bobby's better off for doing it.

I try never to pass up a kid waiting for an autograph after a game unless we lose. Then I just can't bear to stand around trying to be nice when I don't feel like it inside. When I have a public appearance scheduled, then I'll sign them all no matter how I feel—and some kids will bring along a couple of magazine pictures, an autograph book, a puck, a hockey stick and a scrap of paper for an autograph for the little brother.

At first, I don't think I had enough confidence in my own personality to be overly friendly with anybody, especially with total strangers. Within the team, I've always had a good relationship. Outside, although I got to know quite a few people, I always felt they were nice to me mainly because I played hockey and was often in the spotlight. When you're an athlete, if you're around long enough, you get to be in the public eye the year round. It doesn't matter where you go, even if you're on the golf course or in a restaurant, people will say, "There's Stan Mikita, the hockey player." People seem to enjoy seeing you and want to identify themselves with you. I've gotten to know a lot of people this way, and at first I think most were attracted to me by hockey, but eventually this led to personal friendships that will last for life.

Bobby has a natural way of speaking in public, right off the top of his head, and the words seem to come easily to him. I can't work up much enthusiasm for this sort of thing and at first tried to stay away from speaking to groups. I finally tried to make up a speech I could use wherever I went but even that didn't help. I can't stand up there for thirty minutes and keep yacking. I've heard too many people get up in front of a crowd and not only make asses of themselves, but speak for forty minutes and not say two words I really wanted to hear. I prefer just a question and answer period. At least in that way I can be sure people get answers to questions they're really interested in. Or I take a film to a meeting and then have a twenty-minute question and answer period after showing it. I've always felt that if I opened my mouth I wanted something good to come out of it, something constructive, not just a lot of nothing.

It's funny in a way that when you get an image of one sort or another almost everything you do tends to be looked at as in keeping with that image. I remember one day Bill Brennan, a Detroit hockey writer, came up to me when I really wasn't in a bad mood, just a joking mood, and said, "Hi, I'm Bill Brennan of the *Detroit News.*"

"Oh, gee, I'm sorry to hear that," I said, and it took him so far back he was at a loss as to what to say. I apologized later and explained that I had been kidding, since he apparently thought that I was putting him down, probably because I had this reputation for being surly.

It came to a point where I set about deliberately to try and change my off-ice image. I don't know that it was strictly because I realized an athlete with a good image can make a little more money in endorsements, although it certainly hasn't hurt Bobby. I began paying more attention to autograph seekers than I used to, even if I didn't feel great, and maybe I said more to fans after the game than hello; I answered their questions. At the time I thought it was absolutely necessary to do this. Many Americans and Canadians judge an athlete by his public image and I suppose this is not really surprising, though the man inside may not be the same man the public sees and applauds.

Take the case of Joe Namath, the New York Jets quarterback, who had a reputation for being a loudmouth. Well, he backed up his big mouth when the Jets upset the Baltimore Colts in the 1969 Super Bowl game. There are other loudmouths around who can't make their boasts stand up. I've never been a loudmouth, but I've made a point of trying to back up everything I said.

I worked on the image, thinking I might become the All-American boy next door, but I found out it just wasn't in me. Even if I had succeeded in making people believe this was really me I would just have been hoodwinking them. Still, I'm glad I tried it. Just out of the experiment I began thinking more deeply about things than I had, although maturity may have had just as much to do with it. I satisfied something within myself, whether it was my ego, my conscience, or my heart, that I could *appear* to be a guy who always was pleasant, always did the right thing. I found I had the choice of being myself and letting people accept me the way I was or not accept me, which was all right too. I learned that I could be happy with being just exactly the same outside as I was inside and that my family would be happy with me that way, too.

My wife, Jill, never said too much about my efforts in this direction, but I'm sure she only wanted me to be myself because she hates phonies the same as I do.

Bobby could never possibly have had this problem. His great image comes naturally and I think he's just the same inside as outside. More power to him. He's true to himself, which is the way to play it.

The way we play the game, which is quite different, also has to come into the comparison.

I don't know what he thinks about the game. When we lived together those first years as Hawks we were thinking more about girls, although once in a while we might talk hockey. Bobby already was big, whereas I was just a kid coming up. He was after me to shoot more, and he'd say, "Gee whiz, Stan, just keep plugging away. If you shot a little more at the proper time you'd get more goals." At the time I wasn't worried about scoring goals, and I don't know whether I am now or not. It just wasn't my style to play the game like that, although it suited him; I had my own idea of how to play hockey.

But we really never sat down and discussed just what he thought of the game and I don't know how conscientious he was about the game itself or his teammates. We can see a little bit of it in the dressing room or on the ice, but deep down we don't know what he's thinking. It would be pretty tough to get into his mind. I just have to guess.

I don't believe that he thought about the game the same way I did when we were younger. If he did, he didn't show it. He seldom reacted strongly to anything, but I did and I still get nervous before a game. I'm starting to get like Glenn Hall, going to the toilet and throwing up every so often. Nothing seemed to bother Bobby, in hockey or in anything else. I get upset on the ice and if he does, it isn't as apparent. But I'm sure I'm more nervous, maybe because I'm more afraid of failure—of not doing my best, of letting the team down. Whenever I do a job, whatever it is, I like to be serious and do it right. I can fool around off the ice as much as anyone else, but when it comes to doing whatever I have to do, whether it's hockey or even cutting the grass at home, I have to concentrate and do my best. I'm a perfectionist.

Regarding our styles of play, it's really foolish to even compare us as some people try to do. Bobby likes to go behind the net and carry the puck out of his own end zone, get it up somewhere around the other team's blue line and blast away. Naturally, if he's double- or triple-teamed, there's going to be somebody else open, so he'll pass the puck. In my case, I like to get the puck inside our blue line, which gives me thirty, forty, or fifty feet less to get going. But Bobby likes to wind up and this is the way he always has played it and nobody's going to change it now. The same with me, nobody's going to change my style either. We both like to carry the puck, although naturally when you're a center you should have a tendency to pass more often. Also you're in position to pass more when you're going down the middle than on one wing or the other, where you've got only one way to pass—away from the boards. As a wing you can either shoot or pass across the rink. At center, you can go with a pass both ways or take the shot. When you do shoot you've got more of an angle to shoot at from the center of the slot than you have from one of the board angles.

Naturally, the crowd reacts more to Bobby. When you see a player with his speed and power winding up behind the net, going the length of the ice with the puck and busting through, it stands to reason that people are going to get up on their feet with excitement. I'm sure if I started carrying the puck from behind the net and beat two or three of the opposition and got down to the other team's blue line and let a few slapshots go, even if I missed the net and just hit the boards, people would jump up. But I'd just as soon get the puck right at the blue line and walk in and make sure I hit the net.

What it comes down to is that we each get paid to do our own job. Everybody expects Bobby to thrill the crowd with his style and to score goals and he does just that. I really don't know what they expect of me. I've always thought of a center as a playmaker, who's supposed to set up the plays, and if he gets a chance to shoot, he does. I've gotten enough goals. I'm not the lowest-scoring guy in the world and I'm not the highest either, but I think I do my job—shoot when I have a good chance or try to set up somebody else. Both Bobby and I take advantage of our strengths. His forte is that big shot. Mine is to make plays. When you've got something going for you it stands to reason that's what you try to use to your best advantage.

Bobby and I / 99

Things appear in the newspapers in this regard that burn you up. Like near the end of the 1968–69 season, when Bobby had fifty-three goals and was trying to tie his league record of fifty-four. (He finished the season with fifty-eight.) He had scored two goals in a game against Philadelphia in the Chicago Stadium, and in the third period was going for the hat trick as well as goal No. 54. We had the puck on a power play and Bobby was at left point while I was maneuvering around behind the net. The score was 5–2 in our favor at the time and when Kenny Wharram fought his way open in front of the net, I gave him the puck and he put it in on a perfect shot.

The last paragraph in a story about the game said: "Everybody was feeding Hull, but he was being checked so closely on the point that Mikita reluctantly gave the puck to Wharram for an easy tap in." I was really burned when I read that. I thought it was a good play and I think Bobby agreed. Eric Nesterenko gave me the puck, making a good move, and I could have faked a pass to Kenny and shot it, but he maneuvered himself into being wide open, so I flipped the puck to him. It was a legitimate play we'd used on a number of occasions. Any other time it would have been a "picture" play, but now it wasn't so hot because Bobby Hull didn't get the goal. I was pulling for Bobby to get as many goals as he could, but that didn't mean I couldn't appreciate a good play and shot by Kenny. I don't think it's fair that when a writer praises one player or sees everything in a certain light he downgrades another by overlooking or belittling his efforts. Bobby would be the first to agree.

It's true that Bobby and I don't socialize much together any more. You lead a different life after you settle down. We're both married and we each have our own set of friends to go out with or visit after games. As a matter of fact, all the players on the team do. A few years ago, when hockey wasn't as popular in the United States as it is today and people didn't recognize you as readily, you could go out any place with just your teammates. Maybe this is what we still should do—have more team get-togethers. It just seems now that there are too many things happening, the children are getting a little bigger, you want to stay at home more, you have more responsibilities. Still there's no better morale-booster than a team get-together.

I'm still not reluctant to tell Bobby if I think he's doing something wrong on the ice, such as, "You're missing the net too much. At least hit the net with your shot on the power play so we have a chance for the rebound." I can do that without his feelings being hurt and if he has something to say to me I won't feel hurt either. Sometimes you don't realize you're doing something wrong. Another fellow can be a big help. We're not hesitant about these things.

I can guarantee there's no jealousy between us. I don't think there ever has been, either in my case or his.

12

Who's Hurting?

WHEN THE puck went back to Doug Mohns about halfway in from the blue line, I was standing in front of the Pittsburgh net, slightly to one side. Mohns shot, and I was either going to screen for him or deflect the puck into the net, but it hit a defenseman's stick and came right for my eyes. I couldn't duck fast enough so I turned my head and the puck cut my right ear almost in half, leaving the lobe dangling by a thread of flesh.

I was able to skate to our bench and the Hawks looked at the ear and groaned. I started skating toward the exit to the dressing room when the shock hit me and I half-fainted. Assistant trainer Don (Socko) Uren shoved smelling salts under my nose, then half-dragged me to the dressing room. I looked in the mirror to see what the ear was like and almost passed out at the sight of that dangling, bloody mess.

Trainer Nick Garen didn't want to touch the ear because it was such a delicate area and also because he didn't want to be responsible if, after sewing it up, it healed without being perfectly aligned. He sent me to the Pittsburgh Penguins' team physician, who did one helluva good job, first freezing the ear, then sewing the lobe back on with more than twenty stitches. The accident happened on Saturday evening, December 16, 1967, and when we returned to Chicago after the game I was sent to Henrotin Hospital overnight.

We were to play Toronto on Sunday in Chicago and I got out of the hospital that morning, but it wasn't until 6 P.M., later than usual, that I decided to go to the Stadium, although I really wasn't thinking of playing that night.

Habit being what it is, I went down to the dressing room area and was fiddling around in the back room when I had an idea. I yelled for Uren, who also was our equipment manager.

"Sock, get me a steel cup from an athletic supporter," I said.

"Maybe we can figure out some way to use it with this helmet so I can play."

I had worn a helmet part of the previous season after suffering a severe gash near the top of the forehead, but had laid it aside after a while because it was too hot and uncomfortable. Luckily, it was still lying around and now I put it on.

"Don, let's put some protective padding over the ear, put white tape on the cup and invert it over the padding for extra safety," I said. "Then if I wear the helmet I should be able to play."

It took some doing, but we got everything lined up so my ear was protected. The steel cup fit perfectly, not touching the ear at all but resting on my facial bones. Then I went to Coach Reay.

"Billy, if I wear this thing I think I can play tonight," I said.

"I don't know. What if you get hit in the same place?" he said. He thought I was goofy.

"Well, they can sew it up again," I said.

He shook his head, but agreed to let me play. I really don't know what made me want to, other than that it was an important game and we were fighting for first place. Also I figured that even if he just let me sit on the bench I would be more comfortable than up in the stands. As it turned out, it was a tough game, nobody scoring until Pit Martin got a goal for us late in the third period, and soon after I was able to assist on another by Mohns to give us a 2–0 victory over Toronto. The victory moved us into a tie for first place.

I don't think anybody expected me to play, not with the ear in the shape that it was, but maybe I was trying to prove something to myself, although I'm not sure what it was. I know I wasn't trying to prove anything to anybody else, just to myself. I just wanted to play and to win.

I've had my share of injuries, with this one being the ugliest, if not the most serious. But I never used to think much about injuries until I got married and we had children. I wondered: "What on earth am I going to do if I get injured? What's going to happen to my family, how am I going to support them in the same way as now and live the same kind of life?"

We do have several kinds of insurance, but that's only a partial answer. There's a $50,000 term life-insurance policy, with a double indemnity clause in case of accidental death, plus provisions for the loss of an eye, a limb and so on. The club carries insurance to provide medical care if you are injured while playing, and the Players' Association has obtained a major medical plan that covers a player and his family in case of non-service-connected ailments and injuries. We pay half the cost of that, with management picking up the other half. In addition, if you are permanently disabled while playing, the teams usually "take care of you" by providing you with some sort of employment. Still, none of these things can really compensate for the sudden termination of your career as a player by an injury.

I really started thinking about it and I played some games with the thought in mind: "I don't want to get injured." I had to force myself to stop, saying: "Look, you've gone ten years now and there's nothing to say you can't go another ten without getting the kind of injury that would end your career."

Until the last few years I hadn't thought that much about injuries because I had never heard of anybody getting hurt or being crippled too badly to come back to the game. But then Lou Fontinato went into the boards and broke his neck and was paralyzed quite some time, ending his hockey career. I told myself, "Sure, I've got enough insurance, but what good is it if the kids don't have a father?" So, I kept wearing the helmet the rest of the 1967–68 season after my ear healed, and I made up my mind to look around for a better helmet—even make one myself if I had to.

It's hard to say how dangerous hockey is compared with other sports, since I haven't played any others as a professional. I'm sure baseball can be dangerous, especially in plays in which a runner is sliding or when a ball gets away from the pitcher. Football looks violent and I'm sure it's hazardous, but the players are standing on firm ground and are usually butting heads with somebody their own size. When they fall, the ground usually isn't too hard.

Hockey can sometimes be hazardous because the equipment helps make it so—the skates, the sticks, the boards, the goal posts, the puck, and the ice. Yet when you discuss the hazards of hockey, you have to keep in mind that most of the injuries are cuts, muscle pulls, bruises, and charley horses. You see some serious ones once in a while, but surprisingly not that often. A player learns to stay loose to avoid injury and protects critical areas with padding, with the exception of the head—although this is changing. In 1969, when I scored a goal in Montreal, I went into the goal post head first. If I hadn't been wearing a good helmet I would have been lucky to escape with a concussion.

A helmet with a mouthguard attachment, such as the youngsters in organized leagues in Canada and the United States are wearing now, also would have saved my teeth. I've lost three teeth in front, two when Carl Brewer hit me with the butt end of a stick in a Junior-A game, another while with the Black Hawks. I tried wearing a mouthpiece, such as boxers use, but found it too bulky. The mouthguard, attached to the same helmet fastener as the chin strap, lets you use your voice and provides the necessary protection without discomfort, especially if a youngster wears it from the start. I recommend that every youngster use one because teeth are vital to health. It's unfortunate that so many hockey players have lost teeth, and it is foolish to minimize even this kind of injury, although it hardly compares with being slashed by the sharp blade of a skate.

I know what skates can do. I remember an incident with Pat Stapleton when we were both playing for St. Catharines. He had the puck in the corner and fell as he went around behind the net. I was coming from the other side and as he was down on the ice there seemed only one way to avoid him and that was to jump over. My skate caught him in the head, slicing the scalp open; and if the skate had been a little lower, if the toe had hit him in the forehead, it could have been real trouble.

Sticks cause all sorts of damage, but what's really frightening is when they hit somebody around the eyes. In a game at Montreal Jean Beliveau was hit in the eye by a stick and had trouble with his vision for weeks. The newspaper reports were that I had poked him in the eye, when actually I was thirty feet away at the time and didn't even see what happened. I don't know whose stick hit him—in fact, it could have been that of a teammate. I talked to Beliveau about it and he agreed that I wasn't anywhere near him at the time of the incident.

What made the Beliveau affair even worse was what had happened a couple of seasons before to Doug Barkley of Detroit. He lost the vision of an eye and was finished as a player after being hit by Mohns's stick. I was close by when it happened and it was an innocent thing on Mohnsie's part. He lifted his stick, as players do so many times in a game, and he missed Barkley's stick, instead brushing his arm. The stick slid up the arm and caught Barkley squarely in the eye, but at the time I didn't think it was anything critical. This incident made me realize that any injury around the eyes, no matter how trivial it may seem, can be tragic.

You're bound to get some injuries although I've been lucky that none caused me to miss more than a few games. I broke my wrist the first year with the Hawks, which was serious because you're using your hand to earn your livelihood, but not so serious that I couldn't play. I couldn't shoot, but I could pass and maybe tip in the puck.

The dislocated right shoulder I suffered as a junior was about as major as any injury I've had. It required surgery for a second time after my first year with the Hawks because the shoulder had dropped about an inch, a bone sticking up, and everytime I got hit on it or even put on my shoulder pads it became badly irritated. The doctors cut away part of the bone and tied an arm muscle around it to lift the shoulder. When they had finished the right shoulder was even better than the left.

A couple of years later I suffered a broken cheekbone in a game with Toronto when Billy Harris was still with the Maple Leafs. He took a shot from the blue line and when I went down to block it the puck took off and hit me in the cheekbone. That required a little surgical repair, too.

Fractures are always serious but they aren't the most bothersome of injuries. In a way, an ankle sprain can be even worse than a break, because with the fracture the immediate pain is severe, but once the bone is set and a cast is put on you can't move the foot and you give it a proper chance to heal. If you suffer a sprain, you're usually back on the ice before the ankle can heal and the soreness can linger for weeks, even months. The ligaments and tendons are stretched and continually aggravated by the motion of your foot when turning on the ice or taking off.

Seemingly minor injuries can plague you through a whole season; as soon as you get one, another happens. I know that in 1968–69 it seemed as if I was running into one thing or another constantly. I was hit about seven times on one foot by the puck and once on the other and could seldom skate without pain.

Take the left foot, which was injured almost at the start of the season. I had dropped the puck off to Bobby Hull as I crossed the other team's blue line and I figured to wait a fraction of a second, then go into the defenseman and screen the shot for Bobby before getting out of the way after he had time to wind up and fire. Well, Bobby didn't wait. He just cranked the puck and it caught me right in the heel where the heel and sole meet. My heel hurt for the next four months.

Right after that, maybe a game or two later, I stopped a slap shot on the instep of a foot. Then I caught a puck right on the toe, and I lost the nail within a month. Later in the season, I got hit in the back twice by body checks in the first few minutes of a game and developed a muscle bruise or something that forced me to wear a brace on and off the ice and take regular heat treatments for a month.

These injuries kept coming, and they may seem minor but they are hard to shake. They affect your skating and your movement, and at times the bruises can be so severe that you may have to sit out a game or two. That's what happened to me during the 1968–69 season, and I know that I played a lot of games in which I didn't have proper movement because of these injuries.

It might be smarter for players to sit out more games and practices and give injuries a chance to heal rather than rushing right back on the ice as they so often do. If they're not 100%, they usually aren't that much help anyway. But tradition, or whatever the reason, almost forces them to play if they can at all.

For instance, if you get cut, unless it's really bad, you normally go back into action. Even if it's a more painful and disabling injury—a sprained ankle, a charley horse, a pulled groin muscle—I know I always want to try once more to make sure it's serious enough so that I can't really play or that it's only a relative handicap and I can play. It's like the old expression about a drunk getting up the morning after a binge and taking some of the "hair of the dog that bit him." It's the same with a hockey player. If he has a hampering injury, he likes to test himself to make sure he really is hampered.

If it is tradition, maybe it began because when the game first started there were just enough men for both sides and nobody dropped out unless he was dead. I remember my first

Who's Hurting?

year in the NHL when Ted Lindsay, my linemate, was cut under the eye in the first period for twenty-five stitches. By the time he was sewed up, the game was well into the second period and his eye had to be taped open. Ted came back on the ice, played two shifts, then decided he couldn't go on. But I thought that if any player could come out and play like he had after twenty-five stitches, I should be able to play whenever I had a charley horse, or that at least I should try to make a go of it.

The worst injury I ever saw was during a Buffalo-Rochester game in Buffalo. I was still a junior and a spectator. Murray Balfour was playing for Rochester and he had his head down when a man came across the ice and nailed him with a body check, partly with the shoulder and possibly with the elbow. He caught Murray on the side of the head, flipping him over; when he hit the ice he went into convulsions and started to swallow his tongue, but an alert trainer quickly pulled it out, opening his windpipe. I thought he was a goner and it turned out he had a severe concussion.

Kenny Wharram has had a couple of jaw fractures, but those weren't as bad as an incident that happened in an exhibition game. He was hit in the middle of the forehead by a puck, and the skin split wide open. When he was sent to the hospital I called his wife to make sure she didn't hear about his injury first on the late news report.

That's a terrible thing, to call a friend's wife and say, "Your husband's in the hospital. He got hit by a puck square between the eyes. I don't know how serious it is, but I'm calling you so you wouldn't hear about it second hand and jump to worse conclusions."

Later I called her back to tell her that Kenny came out of it with just a slight concussion, but we were all scared to death.

Incidents like these are infrequent, which is why I say hockey is dangerous and it isn't. We're used to the risk. I think hockey looks more dangerous when I'm just watching a game than when I'm playing. A spectator sees a player slammed into the boards, hears the noise, and thinks that the guy must be aching all over. If the check takes place away from the boards, in mid-ice, and you can hear the thud, you know it's a pretty hard check, but it doesn't necessarily mean that the man hit is hurt. If a man is hit with a knee in the thigh he's liable to come up with a charley horse. If he's hit in the shoulder or chest, most of the time he isn't going to be hurt badly but may come out of it with a bruise.

Most of these things you don't feel until the morning after the game, at least that's when they hit me. I can hardly get up the next morning, that's how bad I feel and that's why I like to do push-ups the moment I get out of bed. They wake me up and loosen all the stiff muscles.

I think it comes down to this: hockey isn't especially hazardous if you wear the right protective equipment and haven't got somebody running at you and deliberately trying to injure you. It is hazardous if you've got some nut skating around on the ice. You can draw your conclusions from the fact that I've been hit with solid body checks probably more than anybody else in the league yet have been lucky enough to come out of it with nothing more than an occasional cut or broken bone. I've never been hurt to the point where I couldn't play after missing just a few games. Since I weigh only 165 pounds, hockey can't be as risky as some people make it out to be.

There are exceptional games, though. I remember the final game of the 1966–67 season, against Detroit at the Chicago Stadium. We had already won the championship and the Wings were out of the playoffs, yet it was one of the roughest, toughest games I've been in. They were running around on the ice as if they were trying to maim us, and they succeeded. Bobby Hull suffered a knee injury in a collision with Detroit defenseman Bob Falkenberg, Doug Mohns hurt his back and, worst of all, Matt Ravlich fractured both bones in the lower portion of his left leg.

I really can't believe that the Detroit players were sent out on orders from their coach, Sid Abel, to get us. I like to think the Red Wings were fighting for their jobs next year and maybe this is the way they thought they should have been playing all season, so they tried to make an impression in the last game and overdid it. Still, I remember Bryan Watson of Detroit laughing with glee when Hull was hurt. Watson, who bounced around the league after that, made some sort of reputation at Detroit by being Hull's shadow, although he did it by breaking all the rules and getting away with murder.

I couldn't understand his laughing at Hull's being hurt. I couldn't do that to the man I hated the worst if he got hurt.

Who's Hurting?

I might think, well, he's out of my hair now for a while, but I wouldn't stand around and laugh. Anyway, I never could understand why Bobby let him get away with all that he did for as long as he did, although he finally did crack him a couple of times. I would have given Watson what he had coming to him from the start. I would have figured, why have this guy on my back all season, or two or five seasons, let him know right off the bat that if he wants to check me, fine, but cut out the dirty stuff. I wouldn't have stood for it and eventually Bobby didn't either, but he should have let Watson have a rap or two on the head from the first. That would have decreased the hazards of hockey right then and there.

I can't complain about the travel involved with professional hockey, like some do, although there are times when I get a bit tired of it. But travel is part of the game and you have to put up with some discomforts in order to earn a living. Travel is hectic because the schedules are so tight that you may be playing five games in six nights, or even eight in eleven, as has happened in recent years. But at least most of the trips are just overnight, with only the ones to the West Coast going on for as long as a week. Still, travel in hockey is nothing like in baseball, where a team can be on the road for as long as three weeks.

People often ask why hockey teams lose more often on the road than at home. It's just that some play better in front of a home crowd, getting a lift from having the crowd behind them. Everybody seems to go all out on home ice, whether it's hitting, going into the corners, or skating. Teams are often altogether different on the road. I've noticed that some players can look like King Kong on their home ice but when they come into Chicago they look like they're just padding for a uniform. I hear the crowd when I'm sitting on the bench, but when I'm on the ice I'm usually not aware of it and I think I play the same at home or on the road.

Really, I guess I like travel, the change in scenery, the different sights in different cities. And the game itself isn't routine, there's no plot, each one is exciting and different. I've never thought much about it, but it might take some time for me to get used to a routine nine-to-five job, although I'm sure I would after a while. Unlike some athletes, I couldn't blame a bad game or a bad season on the hardships of travel.

Neither am I going to say that hockey is the most dangerous of sports nor that it's on a level with volleyball as a hazard. It both is and isn't dangerous, and I'm sure most people understand what I mean.

13

Collecting Silverware

I REALLY DIDN'T know all that was in store for me when in late April of 1967 Tommy Ivan telephoned and said, "They want you in Toronto for a publicity luncheon. They're going to award the trophies for the season."

This was after we had won the league championship and Toronto knocked us out of the playoffs in the first round. The Maple Leafs were playing Montreal in the finals and apparently it seemed a good time to hand out the individual season trophies while all the newspaper, radio and TV people were on hand in Toronto. I knew I would be getting the Ross Trophy as scoring champion because that's cut and dried. I'd had ninety-seven points—although I honestly knew it was ninety-eight. And the Ross Trophy was really all that I was expecting when I went to Toronto. Since it meant going for just a day, I took Jill and our daughter Meg along.

The affair was held in a banquet room in Maple Leaf Gardens and on the way in I met Harry Howell of New York and Bobby Orr of Boston. It already had been announced that Howell had won the Norris Trophy as the outstanding defenseman and that Orr had been selected for the Calder Trophy as rookie of the year. I congratulated them and Howell reminded me to sit next to him at the head table.

"What on earth is going on here?" I asked Harry. "We didn't have all this the other times I got the Ross Trophy."

"This is a little special," said Harry. "They're going to present you with trophies, not the trophy."

"What are you talking about? Which trophies?"

"You won the three trophies," said Harry, who apparently had been informed by his team about how the trophies were being distributed while I hadn't been told by my club.

I was astounded, then pleased, and I can't express all the emotions that went through me. It was unbelievable. Naturally, I knew I had a chance for the Lady Byng for sportsmanship because I had behaved myself during the season, getting only twelve minutes in penalties. And since the Black Hawks had won the Prince of Wales Cup there was a good chance one of us would get the Hart Trophy as the league's most valuable player. But I had figured the best a guy could do is get one or the other. It just hadn't occurred to me that a player could win all three, mainly I guess because it had never been done before. I was nearly knocked off my feet, and I began wondering what to say when they called on me. Luckily, as Clarence Campbell, president of the league, introduced me, he said something about winning three trophies in a season being quite a feat "for a young man who came from Czechoslovakia." This rang a little bell in my head, reminding me of what the kids used to call me and a remark Jill had made earlier. I got up, thanked everybody and came to the punch line.

"Well, as my wife said to me before I walked into this room, this isn't bad for a little DP." Everybody laughed and I think it was accepted in the right kind of way.

As I said before, I don't think I'll be able to fully appreciate what these trophies mean to me until some day when I'm no longer playing and can look back on my career. Maybe when I'm sixty I'll be sitting and having a beer with some crony and I'll say, "By crackie, I couldn't have been too bad a player, look at all this silverware."

What I'm trying to say is that I appreciate all these trophies, the Ross four times in five years and the triple trophies in 1967–68 as well as in 1966–67, but I also need time to think about just what they mean. Right now, I'm in the thick of things and every season, every game is a challenge.

Hockey, being a team game, one player can't really take credit for a scoring title because you owe so much to the entire club and in particular to your two wingers. Since I like to pass the puck, the only way I can get a lot of assists is if the people I'm playing with are in the right spot to score. They have to have a talent of their own, first of all to get in the right place and secondly to put the puck in the net. Also, I get a few goals here and there, which means not only that I can shoot and get in the right place but that the men I play with have the skills to get the puck to me. It's all teamwork and one player really can't win a scoring title on his own.

Collecting Silverware / 113

I don't rate goals over assists. I've gotten more satisfaction at times out of getting three assists on a hat trick by a line-mate like Kenny Wharram than out of scoring myself. I felt much happier for him because it meant more to Kenny than to me to score a goal. He is expected to score goals, it's more his job than it is mine. A center is supposed to set up the play and it's up to the wing to get in the right place and knock the puck into the net.

I know that much more emphasis is placed on goals than on assists by some writers and fans, but both are equally important. After all, a player that passed to the goal-scorer might have had to beat two or three coming down the ice, then had to get into good position for a pass to the wing who is standing in front of the net for a tip-in. Now who gets the credit, the man who did all the work or the one who scored the goal? You know the answer.

Then there are cases in which the assist might just have consisted of passing off to a player in your own end. The man with the puck then worked his way through the whole opposing team to go in and score. In this case, the player who scored the goal deserved the credit. That's why it's hard to generalize on assists and goals. Sometimes the goal is more of a feat, other times the assist.

I never placed much emphasis on trying to win any of the four scoring titles until the last three weeks of the season. Too many things could happen until then—being injured, going into a slump, or some other player getting hot. But when it got near the wire, I made a conscious effort to make sure of the title.

The final games of the regular season in both 1966–67 and 1967–68 were something special in different ways because of the scoring races. In the first instance, it wasn't really a question of whether I'd lead the league in scoring, because I had a comfortable margin going into the final game at New York. At that time the record for total points was held by Bobby Hull, who had set it the year before with ninety-seven. I went into the final game with ninety-five points and picked up two assists to tie the record, but I think I should have received a third one.

I had been standing in front of the net when the puck went back to the point and one of our men slapped it. I deflected the puck, it went over the net, hit the glass, bounced back over the net to Doug Mohns, who got it past the goalie for his twenty-fifth goal of the season. I should have been credited with an assist because I was the last to touch it before Mohnsie, but the official scorer didn't see me get a stick on the puck. So, instead of ninety-eight points, I ended the 1966–67 season with ninety-seven, and instead of breaking the record, I tied it.

I tried to say that it didn't mean anything to me, but it really did. I wanted the scoring record for one reason—nobody could beat it until the next March 31. To grab something for one hour, one day, one year means something at a particular moment. Not that you think you're going to hold onto it. I knew somebody else would come along in a year, two or three and break the record. And, of course, Phil Esposito did smash it out of recognition three years later when he got 126 points. That record will be broken too sooner or later. Hockey players seem quicker and bigger than ever, and the game has changed, with everybody more offensive-minded. Naturally, the records are going to be broken almost year by year. Still, you like to have them for a moment. So I was upset at the time, but not to the point where I hung my head and cried in my beer.

The 1967–68 scoring title meant even more to me because the race was the closest of any and it went down to the last day. Going into the final game, against Detroit at the Stadium, I had eighty-four points; Gordie Howe of the Red Wings had eighty-one, and Phil Esposito, by then traded to Boston, had eighty-three. I wasn't as concerned about beating out Howe as I was about staying ahead of Esposito, because Phil had been on our club and the critics had been howling about what a bad trade the Hawks had made in sending him to Boston along with Fred Stanfield and Ken Hodge in exchange for Pit Martin, Gilles Marotte, and Jack Norris. Some of us were just as sick and tired of hearing all this criticism of the trade as our management must have been. I figured if Phil beat me in the scoring race on top of it, we would never hear the end of it, so I had to stay ahead of him to save face for somebody.

I almost hoped Howe would tie me in total points, so great was my admiration for the man. The day of the game was his fortieth birthday and here he was battling for a scoring title and had a chance to end the season with forty goals. It was amazing. Still, I wanted to beat him, as I had a three-point edge on him and since we were playing against each other, I knew exactly where he stood at any given moment. But Esposito was just a point back and Boston was playing at home against Toronto, which increased his chances of picking up some points.

I was a little shaky when the game started, but as it went along I settled down. In the second period I picked up an assist on a goal by Wharram, then added another early in the third period on Mohns's goal. I needed them, too, because at intermission I had heard that Esposito had scored at least a goal in Boston. I didn't know what else he might be doing.

As for the game itself, Detroit was leading 5–4 with about five minutes left. That's when Mohns passed to me at right point and I thought I'd try something I had been thinking about all day.

In a game between New York and Montreal televised that afternoon, Camille Henry of the Rangers had bounced the puck past the goalie on a sort of lob shot. I had been watching the game with Bobby Schmautz, and Henry's goal set me thinking.

"Nine years I've been shooting like that in practice and I've never yet done it in a game," I told Bobby. "You watch, I'm going to put one in like that."

"Well, you could do it with a little luck," said Schmautz. "I've seen you try it in practice and I've tried it myself a few times. The puck can do a lot of strange things. It just might work."

This kind of shot from center ice is a goaltender's nightmare because there is no way of figuring which way it will bounce and it's really just a matter of out-guessing the puck, which seems to have a mind of its own.

When I got the pass from Mohns I lofted the puck in on Roger Crozier, the Detroit goalie, and with a couple of crazy hops it went right past him into the net. That tied the game at 5–5, gave me my fortieth goal—the most I've had in a season—and clinched the scoring championship. With eighty-seven points, I finished three ahead of Esposito and five ahead of Howe.

Howe was quoted as saying after the game that I had earned the title, that I hadn't backed in, but I really don't think that made a difference. Even if neither one of us picked up points that night it wouldn't have meant that we had played a bad game. You can play well without getting any points, something that's frequently overlooked.

Without hesitation I'd have to choose the Most Valuable Player award as the greatest honor I've received. This is the Oscar of hockey. It means that people consider you the best player in the league out of more than two hundred—whether you are or not—and there can't be any higher praise. That I was selected twice is just unbelievable to me.

On the subject of awards, there's something I would like to clear up, especially because a lot of people wrote letters to me after I failed to attend the awards ceremonies in Montreal in 1967–68, the second year I won three trophies. Some of the mail was favorable, but a lot of it wasn't, and I know the league officials weren't too happy with me.

Traditionally, the award ceremonies were held after completion of the playoffs, so when the Black Hawks had been knocked out early, I took my family on a vacation in Florida. We had planned a trip for some time, and originally even thought of going out of the country. I wasn't told that the ceremonies would be held during the playoffs until Wednesday, the second day we were in Florida and two days before they were going to take place in Montreal. This meant I had to leave Florida and catch a plane Thursday, to make sure I'd be in Montreal by Friday morning. As I always am after a season ends, I was pretty beat, emotionally and physically, and it was easy to become angry at not being notified earlier. I didn't want to leave my wife and children and I decided not to go. Jill was also put out, but after thinking it over urged me to go anyway, saying I owed it to the fans if nobody else. Still it didn't seem fair not to give a player some reasonable advance notice, and I didn't attend the ceremonies and only later realized I had made a mistake. No matter how legitimate my reasons, I should have attended and then voiced my opinions about giving the players a little more consideration. It put me in a bad light, as though I felt I was really hot stuff and couldn't be bothered. Actually, I don't know if there's any other player who recognizes more how much he owes hockey.

Some of the press was sympathetic with my view, though, realizing what it meant for an athlete to be able to spend more time with his family after having been away from home so much for the previous seven months.

Later I apologized to Campbell, telling him I used bad judg-

Collecting Silverware / 117

ment in not going and was sorry about it; but whether he fully accepted my apology, I'm not sure. I also apologized to as many people as I could, but after judgment has been passed it's almost impossible to make amends.

Over the years I made the All-Star team as first-string center six times and the second team once, and naturally it was gratifying. Still, I was a little hurt in 1968–69 when I missed making even the second team at mid-season and only got in the All-Star Game because I was chosen among the extra men by Toe Blake, coach of the East team. I couldn't blame anybody for not picking me first. Esposito was having a great season and you couldn't dispute his selection as the No. 1 center. But as much as I admired Jean Beliveau of Montreal, I thought I could have been chosen second All-Star in place of him, or at least received some support in the voting, especially as I had the edge in goals and points.

I've played in a few All-Star Games and have always considered them as real contests. That's the way most of us play them, because you owe it to the fans and because you're more likely to get injured if you try to be overly careful. It's also a tremendous honor, and certainly the high point of the games I've been in has to be the one in 1967 against Montreal because I played on a line with Howe and Bobby Hull. I considered Bobby the greatest left winger in hockey and Howe the greatest right winger and all-around player. Yet playing with them made it the toughest game I've ever played in my life. Both of them liked to skate so much off their wings that I didn't know where to go. I just tried to keep out of their way, and if the puck happened to come to me, I took it as far as possible, then passed it off to one of them. I didn't touch the puck three times all night and Howe and Bobby were whizzing across me like hornets.

There's no doubt league honors meant a lot to me, but it would be unfair to overlook some that came from other, unofficial sources and perhaps were just as important in their way. It's gratifying to be named the player of the year by the sporting magazines, and I've been fortunate to get such recognition.

Also, every year the Stand Bys, a club of Black Hawk fans, holds an awards banquet, and to the players it's one of the greatest events of the season. I know I've always enjoyed them and Glenn Hall, when he was with the Hawks, always got a tremendous kick out of the parties.

The Stand Bys give two awards, one for high points on the team, which is like the Ross Trophy, and another to the most valuable player of the Black Hawks. This particular MVP trophy has to be one of the finest awards a player can receive, because it's determined by the vote of his teammates. (The sports writers in the league choose the NHL's MVP winner.) Here you were, playing with seventeen men, and the majority of them considered you the fellow that contributed most to keeping the club going that season. There could be no finer tribute, because it came from the players who knew best how much you did or didn't contribute.

Whenever I got that Stand By MVP trophy I couldn't help thinking, "This is pretty good too for a little DP."

14

The Hired Hand

IT TOOK ME a while to realize I could be well paid for playing hockey, but once the idea got across I made certain I got my due. Fans might think it's glamorous and more play than work, but being a professional is a job and an athlete is a hired hand just like anyone else working for a living.

When I was a rookie, Ted Lindsay gave me advice that I never overlooked while negotiating a contract or making a deal, whether in hockey or business.

"I don't care what kind of contract you're signing," said Lindsay, "whether it's in hockey or some other field, make sure you're satisfied with it. Don't sign unless you can live with the deal. In hockey, don't play for peanuts but don't expect some astronomical figure because you're not going to get it. Be proud but reasonable in everything."

This became my philosophy. I never signed a contract that I wasn't satisfied with at the time of agreement, although as the season or seasons went on I might have regretted doing so. All my hockey contracts during the first ten years, except the one I signed in 1968, were for more than one season, which led to some regrets before they ran out. There were times while bound to a contract that I thought the results management was getting from me were more than they were paying for. At times I thought about asking for a raise, but didn't do it because I had voluntarily bound myself to the terms.

Still, I couldn't help thinking, "I'm bound to this contract, but they could change it on their own if they wanted to. They could come to me and say, 'Stan, we want to give you a raise. We think you deserve it.' "

I had heard of other teams doing this, as Detroit did with Howe in 1968, but it never happened to me with the Black Hawks. The first season I won the three trophies I was in the middle of a three-year contract and that was one time I definitely felt it would have been a nice gesture on management's part to give me an increase. I thought about this each time a contract expired, and added a little more to my demands than I would have otherwise.

I did all my own negotiating with Tommy Ivan the first nine years and he was a tough man to bargain with, although I can hardly compare because I never dealt with anybody else.

I always set a figure for myself that I would be satisfied with. Before I started to negotiate, I sat down and figured out what I thought I was worth to the club and what I hoped to contribute the next season. I kept it realistic. I had heard of players asking for $50,000, then settling for $20,000. I couldn't see the point of that.

I never compared my salary with anybody else's. I didn't know what they were getting and I didn't care. It was none of my business. But I did think hockey players were underpaid in comparison with other professional athletes. Partly it was because we came from Canada and we thought in terms of what our neighbors in other occupations were getting, which was something less than people in the United States got for the same jobs. We didn't put ourselves at the proper level and maybe were satisfied with too little. Then, too, every youngster in Canada dreamt of playing on an NHL team, and with just six teams until recently, the owners had a big surplus of talent to draw from and were more in the driver's seat. We should have compared ourselves with other professional athletes—or as "entertainers," we should have asked for the salaries of entertainers. Eventually we did.

By 1968 I knew athletes in other sports were getting contracts calling for $60,000, $75,000, and even $100,000 a year. In fact, $100,000 became almost a common salary. It seemed to me that fellows who contributed as much to hockey as athletes like Joe Namath and Bart Starr did to football and Frank Robinson and Mickey Mantle did to baseball should be much better paid.

What made everything clear to me was the contract offer I received in the summer of 1968. I was coming off my second triple trophy after the expiration of a three-year contract and the Hawks sent me a piece of paper calling for what in effect was a pay cut. The total money was slightly more, but as the hockey schedule by this time had increased from 70 games to

76 and the cost of living had gone up considerably, I was actually offered a cut in pay.

I decided that I couldn't get anything like the kind of money athletes in other sports got by negotiating on my own as I had done. So I went to Mark McCormack of International Management, Inc., the man who handles the affairs of Arnold Palmer, Jack Nicklaus, Jean-Claude Killy and others. I figured McCormack had helped to make Palmer a millionaire, and while I didn't expect to reach that status, I could also get a lot of help with investments and money management. It worked out that way. These people negotiated my contract for me in 1968 and put me on a budget, and they've made investments for me. The final decisions are still mine, but I think it makes sense for an athlete to get expert help in handling his financial affairs because there'll come a time when he can no longer capitalize on his skills in sports.

Before leaving the subject of money, I'd like to say something about bonuses for performance, a common part of hockey contracts. When I was a kid I thought that what a player didn't get on his regular pay schedule he could make up in bonuses. I had a deal in one contract in which I was paid $500 as a bonus if I got 20 goals or 50 points, $500 more if I got 25 goals or 60 points and another $500 if I got 30 goals or 70 points. But I came to the conclusion that bonuses of this sort were harmful. We were getting paid a salary for doing a job, and should be satisfied with that income. I don't think we needed a bonus to get up for each game.

Also, bonuses can lead to point and goal hunting near the end of a season, and even dissension on a team. This happened to the Hawks. There was an instance when goalkeeper Glenn Hall was going for the Vezina Trophy at the end of the season. If he won it, he had a good bonus coming. At the same time, there were a couple of other players who had bonuses coming for goals or points and needed just two or three in that last game. All we had to do for the Vezina was to hold the other club to three goals or less, which meant that if we forechecked in their zone and lined up at the center-ice red line and kept dumping the puck back, we could do it easily. But since some were going for their scoring bonuses, we couldn't play it that way and as a result, we had a wild scoring game. Some of the players got their $500 for points or goals, but

Hall was out about $5,000, which he would have collected from the league and the club for the Vezina.

The only kind of bonus I believe in would be one to each player for the team making the playoffs. After all, if a club makes the playoffs, management is guaranteed income from at least two extra home games. They should be more than willing to give this type of bonus because they would be getting it back at the gate. The playoffs are the clubs' bonus and they should be the players' bonus, too, a reward for team effort, which after all is what hockey is all about.

Just one more thing about pay. Most of the things that the newspapers print about salaries are way off the mark. I don't know where the writers get the figures, they're so wild. I didn't know what Bobby Hull was getting in the 1968–69 season after his one-day "retirement," and I had no idea of how the writers arrived at the figures they printed about this salary. I frankly didn't care what he was getting because I was satisfied with my arrangement and the newspaper stories didn't mean a thing to me.

What does mean something to me is the upgrading of hockey salaries all along the way, so that they are brought more into line with what other professional athletes earn. There has been a lot of progress in this since the league expanded to twelve teams in 1967, but there could be more—with owners now receiving television income, increased money from concessions due to growing fan interest, and higher ticket prices. And the same goes for other fringe benefits, such as training-camp pay and conditions, pensions, insurance, and travel standards. I have always approved of the Players' Association's aims to unify—not "unionize"—the people in hockey. As Hawk player representative to the Association as well as to the Pension Society, I think I did my share in the effort to upgrade standards.

All these things played a part in keeping me in closer contact than the average player with the club brass. I learned to understand their problems, too. Although Ivan and I never hit it off too well in the salary area, I could appreciate that the role of a general manager is a difficult one. He's the middleman in at least two ways. On contracts he represents the owners to the players, and he's also between the coach and the owners. It's not a job I would crave.

I'm not so sure I would ever want to coach, either. I played

The Hired Hand

for two men, Rudy Pilous and Billy Reay, during my first ten years as a Black Hawk and both had their problems. There were times when I thought that if I were running the club I would do this or that, but when it came right down to it I realized that the coach was trying just about everything he could and that I really hadn't come up with anything new. And you can be sure that when things aren't going well it's easier to get rid of one man—the coach—than eighteen players.

Pilous was coaching the team my first four years and he knew his stuff, leading us to the Stanley Cup in 1960–61, but I don't know that he really won the team's respect in the long haul. At times he treated us like teenagers, maybe because so many of us had played for him as juniors at St. Catharines. He didn't seem to realize that five, six years later we had become men. He didn't seem to think us capable of making decisions or of doing certain things without being nagged, and I know many players resented it.

What really hampered Pilous was his difficulty in handling the team as a group, which was ironic because he knew how to get along with most of the members individually. The friction mounted as the seasons went by. I can't really pin it down but it seems to me that he lost control of the situation; he was too nice a guy and let too many things slide by. As a result he was fired after the 1962–63 season and Billy Reay, former Montreal center, was brought in to coach.

When Reay took over he was a tough disciplinarian who demanded that things be done his way, or else. He treated everybody the same and rightly demanded the best at all times. If a player made a mistake Reay let him know about it right then and there, whether it was privately or in front of the club. He would really chew us out, saying, "You're not doing your job. If you don't want to do it get the hell out of here." Reay wasted no time in straightening someone out, and if the player refused to be straightened, off he went.

But over the years Billy Reay mellowed quite a bit. Whether for better or worse I wasn't sure, though the way things turned out in 1968–69 when we finished sixth, some people will feel it couldn't have been for the better. I'm not fingering Billy or anyone else for the last-place finish. If a team sinks in the standings it falls on the players' shoulders.

After a few seasons, instead of letting a player know just

what he thought of him right then and there, Billy was waiting a day or two before taking him aside and talking to him privately. Perhaps it was the smarter way. Coaches have to be masters of psychology and treat each player in a different way depending on how he reacts to criticism.

Still, when Reay first came he didn't hold back as much and really roasted someone who wasn't doing his job. The players seemed to respond more when he was like that. I guess a coach can be friendly, but he also has to be a stern disciplinarian. I think Billy kept things too much bottled up inside after the first few years, and he and the players both might have been better off if he had kept on blasting them as he did at the start. With all that, Billy was a fine coach and a likeable man, and we got along together fine.

Reay has a great advantage in that he was a top NHL player himself, as a center for the Montreal Canadiens in the late 1940s and early '50s. He knows all the technical aspects of the game and as a former player is able to communicate them convincingly to his players. He has the background and the knowledge of hockey that make for a smooth relationship between coach and players, with both sides striving to get along.

I can't quite say the same about getting along all the time with Clarence Campbell, not that the league president showed as much by his actions as by his attitude that he disapproved of me. But ever after that incident in which I banged into referee Vern Buffey, he didn't seem to have much use for me. I don't know whether he didn't want to get too close to the players because of the nature of his duties or what the reason was, but he always seemed cool. Sure, I could go up to him and say hello and exchange a few words, but it never went beyond that—not that I expected any special consideration. Yet I always thought that if I needed advice I could ask him for it and he'd give it to me sincerely and straight down the line. In the situation in which he arbitrated my salary dispute with Ivan he backed me, although I wondered if this was some kind of game he and Tommy were playing with me; whether I was just the middleman in a squeeze. Maybe the thought was unfair, but we always considered Campbell an owners' man because, after all, they chose and paid him.

What it really comes down to is that I was never sure of how to view Campbell either as league president or as a man, he seemed so cool, so detached—which may have been his na-

The Hired Hand

ture. I know that my decision not to show up for the triple trophy awards ceremony in 1968 didn't endear me to him despite my later apology.

My relationship with the owners of the Black Hawks was never very close, although I knew them a little better than some players know the people who pay their salaries, but not as well as others do.

I did have the opportunity and good fortune to get to know Jim Norris, one of our owners, before he died in 1966. Although he was a millionaire many times over, he was a regular guy in every sense of the term. He treated the players as his equals and when he talked to you he didn't beat around the bush, he told you what he thought and he expected the same from you. Wealthy as he was, he was a plainspoken man and as enthusiastic about hockey as a second-balcony fan. Win or lose, he'd come down to the dressing room after a game. If we lost, he'd never say a word, just walk into the coach's office. If we won, he'd just come in, say "Good game, boys," and walk out again. He also knew how to have a good time. When we won the Stanley Cup he threw a terrific party and he got just as smashed as we did. We really missed him after he was gone.

In many ways Billy Wirtz, who moved in after a while to run the club for his dad, Arthur M. Wirtz, represented the same kind of man that Jim Norris had been, and not only as a hockey fan. Although highly educated, Billy Wirtz was able to talk the players' language. He was a worthy successor to Jim Norris in that he always levelled with you. Just like Jim, Billy was a true hockey fan as well as an owner and could be counted on to treat the players with consideration. Any time I've dealt with Billy I've always been sure of getting a fair shake.

15

A Man's Family

MY WIFE, JILL, is never afraid to speak her mind, which is one of the many reasons I was attracted to her. She and the rest of the players' wives were disturbed a couple of times when Ivan and Reay decided to take the team to a resort hideaway ninety miles from Chicago for the duration of the Stanley Cup playoffs. Management had the idea that a player had so many distractions and so many errands to run when he was home that he couldn't keep his mind on the game and was too worn out from running around to do his job on the ice. I didn't agree with that and neither did Jill.

"If they don't want the players to be bothered by their families, why don't they send their wives and kids to the resort for a vacation and let you stay home?" she suggested. "We're all right for you seventy games of the year, but when the playoffs come we're no good for you."

Leave it to Jill to come up with a clever idea—and she was partly right. In my view nothing could be further from the truth than that a happy family life wasn't one of the greatest tonics a player could have. I liked to get my mind off hockey during the day and my wife and children were a perfect out for me. I couldn't think of a better way to relax on game day than to play with the children, read them a story, take a walk with them, or even feed and diaper the baby. Besides, being on the road as much as we were, it was a difficult life for Jill at home. She had to be with the youngsters twenty-four hours a day while we were gone. When I was home one of the greatest things I could do for her was to baby-sit while she went shopping. I knew it was going to cost me a little money but she was happy as a lark when she got home.

I first met Jill during the latter part of the 1961–62 season when she was working as a secretary to Congressman Harold Collier of the eleventh district of Illinois. A friend invited me

A Man's Family

to a testimonial dinner for Representative Collier. Since the dinner was taking place the same night as a Stand By Club banquet I wasn't sure if I could make it, but I said I'd try to be over later. It was lucky for me I decided to go, although I could hardly be sure of that the first moment I met Jill. A mutual friend, Mickey Madigan, introduced us.

"Jill, this is Stan Mikita . . . this is Jill Cerny," he said.

After a polite nod, "Excuse me," said Jill, then took off just like that, and I didn't see her for an hour. I didn't know what to think. Finally, I sat down at a table with Bobby and Joanne Hull and watched the floor show. I propped my feet on a chair and all of a sudden Jill came back, knocked my feet off the chair and said, "Well, I'm back, excuse me." She sat down and added, "I'll have a Scotch now."

It was love at first sight for me. I looked at her and thought, there's the girl I'm in love with. At first it was her beauty, but later it was a lot of other things. She was so attractive, with dark brown hair and brown eyes and a straightforward manner, that I knew right away this was the girl for me. I had never been serious about a girl before and all of a sudden one look and that was it—right out of a Hollywood script.

Jill went to Washington soon after we met, to work in the Congressman's office. She came back periodically and we had a couple of dates, and the summer of 1962 I went to visit her in Washington. Then I took her to visit my parents, the Mikitas, in St. Catharines. I showed her around the town and as we looked into Murray Walters' jewelry store window she happened to mention she liked a marquis-cut diamond. I was too stupid to know if she was hinting, but after she returned to Washington I went into the store and picked out an engagement ring with a marquis-cut diamond. Fortunately, it turned out to be the right size.

A few weeks later I visited her in Washington, with the ring in my pocket. She dragged me along to a political dinner, one of those $100-a-plate things, and it seemed the evening would never end. Afterwards, we ended up at the apartment she shared with some other girls. Her mother was there on a visit, and Jill had invited Congressman Collier and his son Cal in for a drink. Everybody sat around and talked and it seemed as if they'd never go home. And here I was with a ring burning a hole in my pocket. It was three o'clock in the morning before they left and I was half asleep, impatient to get back to my hotel.

"Listen, do you want to get married or not?" I blurted. "If you do, here's the ring. That's it. I'm going back to the hotel."

She was taken aback. I mean, it wasn't exactly the way a girl imagines getting a proposal.

"Well, I don't know," she said, sort of shocking me in turn. I had to do some fast talking, but finally she said, "Well, we'll get engaged."

Jill was twenty and I was twenty-three when we were married the next spring, on April 27, 1963, at St. Mary of Celle Church in Berwyn, Illinois, a suburb of Chicago.

She was born in Oak Park and raised in Berwyn and Cicero, all western suburbs a few miles apart. Her father is of Czech descent, her mother of Irish, and she was the middle child of three in the family, with her brother Jack a couple of years older and her sister Peggy three years younger. Her father Charles is a welder and a great sports enthusiast. Her mother's name is Margaret, and we named our first child, born February 2, 1964, after her, also giving Meg the middle name of Anne, after my mother in St. Catharines. Our son, Scott, was born March 8, 1966, and our second daughter, Jane Elizabeth, arrived on February 3, 1969.

Life changed in a lot of ways after we were married. For one thing, suddenly I had a large family in the Chicago area because Jill has many relatives. And it was a wonderful thing. Two or three times a year we all got together either at our house or one of theirs. We always had the annual Christmas party at our house and I know nobody enjoyed it more than I did.

Jill's dad, Chuck, turned out to be more of a friend than a father-in-law. We spent a lot of time together golfing, having a few beers, taking the kids to the zoo or somewhere else for recreation. My mother-in-law, Marge, is a fine cook and for a long while after we were first married we had dinner there once a week.

Jill had gone a couple of years to the University of Illinois, majoring in physical education, before she took the job with Congressman Collier, and she soon urged me to go back to school in the summers and at least finish high school. But one thing or another always intervened and soon our family was growing and I began having business interests.

Still, I was learning in the school of life, and just as I'm different today from when I was twenty, I expect I'll be wiser and hold somewhat different views in another ten years. Like all young marrieds, before Meg was born we had been free to do pretty much what we wanted to, just pick up and go when we felt like it. After Meg came, at first we felt tied down because we couldn't hit the town with the other players and their wives after the games, but it was near the end of the season and the next fall Meg made it easier for us. She began to walk at eight months and—I guess every parent thinks this of their child—began acting in a way that made it easier for us to leave her with a good baby-sitter. Then the second child came and the third and that cut our social activities to a minimum.

Nevertheless I enjoyed family life and its responsibilities and pleasures from the start. Not so much (at times) during the season because I still got too wrapped up in hockey. But once the season was over I couldn't think of a better way to spend a day than with the children. Not that I made it a point to spend that time with them. I felt it had to be a mutual feeling, that if I wanted them and they wanted me at any particular time we should read together, roll on the floor, or do whatever we felt like doing.

At first I was stricter with the children than I should have been, and for a while I let them upset me more than they should have, but I calmed down after a time; I was growing up with them. Perhaps I was over-strict at first because I had met too many youngsters who had forgotten or never learned some simple courtesies, such as using a common word in our language, one of six letters, "please." And a three-letter word "yes," which they didn't use too often, instead saying "yeah" or "yep." I wanted my kids to come up to people and say "Yes, please . . . no, thank you"—to be polite, well-behaved, and well-mannered, but more important, never to get the idea at home or elsewhere that they were special because Daddy's picture was in the paper or people saw him on television. Our entire home life, as a matter of fact, is as unpretentious as possible, with all the publicity and ballyhoo left behind. Jill has both feet on the ground and runs the house much like any suburban housewife, and I catch just as much heck because I'm late for supper, forget to pick up some milk, or come up with excuses when the windows need washing. I wouldn't trade our home life for anything.

I also began thinking more about the future, how to provide my family with a good living and a good education even if I could no longer play hockey. I'd like to see them go to college if they want to, especially my son Scott—not that I'm against girls going to college, but I don't think it's so important for them.

I'd have no objection to Scott's becoming a hockey player if that's what he wanted to do. I'd even give him advice if he asked, but I wouldn't push him towards the game because I'd want him to get his education first. I put him on skates before he was two, and Meg started when she was one and a half. I never tried to teach them to skate, leaving that up to the instructors; besides, they never listened to me when it came to showing them how to do something. Even with toys, if I tried to help them they'd say, "No Daddy, I'll do it myself." I couldn't object, because in my childhood I was the same.

Jill had seen a few hockey games before we were married, but afterward the only time she ever missed one was when a pregnancy interfered. She usually sat with her mother and Nancy Maki, Chico's wife, and whomever Nancy took. Of course, I never knew how she reacted when I was on the ice, and I was too busy to look at her and see.

She would mention once in a while that her mother would get excited and I asked her, "What about you? Don't you get excited?"

"I don't know," she said. "I keep doing my crossword puzzles. Once in a while I look up."

I knew very well she was watching me all the time I was on the ice and every play that went on, though we seldom talked much about a game after it was over. Once in a while she would say something critical. If it was about me, fine. If it was about somebody else on the club I would say, "Forget it. Tell me about it tomorrow because I don't want to hear it now." I figured if she wanted to rap me, O.K., and if she wanted to pat me on the back that was all right too. But if she started doing it with somebody else, maybe she should have been out there coaching.

I don't know how much she resented criticism of me by fans or sportswriters, but I think she realized I tried to do my best, that sometimes it was good enough, at other times it wasn't. I know there were times she'd read or hear something and flare up.

"Who the heck do they think they are that they know so much about the game!" she'd say, although usually she wouldn't mention something to me that she happened to overhear. But if she read something in a newspaper that she didn't like she'd burst out, "What on earth is this? That guy is ridiculous! What he's writing is crazy. He's an idiot!"

Sometimes I'd agree at least partially with the writer and that really got her boiling. But we never discussed a particular game or the people on the club too much and I really never knew how much the players' wives gossiped about each other's husbands. I never asked.

Generally, Jill didn't seem to worry about injuries. She realized that in the long history of the game there seldom have been truly serious injuries and that only one man had been killed in fifty years of National Hockey League play. She knew that I could take care of myself and that I wasn't going to start swinging a stick at somebody and have somebody swinging a stick at me, about the most dangerous thing that could happen.

If during a game I got cut up badly enough to leave the ice and go to the dressing room, I always made it a point to come back for at least one shift so she'd know I wasn't so badly hurt that she had to worry. If the injury was more serious, I tried to get word to her one way or another as soon as possible and, if we were on the road, I'd call her right after the game.

Some hockey wives are phone hounds—they call their husbands no matter where they may be and never stop talking. Jill isn't like that. She didn't like to call me on the road, especially if she had bad news, because she didn't want me to worry when I really couldn't do anything about a situation anyway. Of course, if there was something wrong with the kids when I left home, she'd phone to let me know how they were, or I'd call her; but otherwise she tried never to call me unless there was good reason.

As I said, when the children came along it cut down our social life pretty much. In the first place, I liked to be home with the family, especially if the kids were good. I didn't mind their climbing on me even if I were aching all over after a game, although if they were whining or crabbing I'd just as soon not be around, but I learned to live with that, too.

As for going out on the town together, we did that less and less frequently. As I became better known and hockey boomed in the United States it got to be more and more difficult to go somewhere people didn't recognize me and ask for autographs. If we went to a restaurant or night club somebody would be sure to ask to sit with us and what could I say? I had to be polite. I couldn't tell them that we might want to be by ourselves that evening.

Every summer we try to go somewhere for a weekend or take a couple of weeks' vacation, somewhere I hope we won't be recognized and can have a rest and time to ourselves; but we can't always be sure. One year, during the season, we had a week between games and the coach said it would be all right if I skipped practice. Jill and I went to Boca Raton, Florida. One night we went to see a show featuring Debbie Reynolds at a hotel in Miami Beach. We had a table up front and before we knew it people were coming up to ask me for autographs. I would expect that in Chicago or even in Toronto, but in Florida!

What made it sort of funny was that Steve Lawrence and Eydie Gorme were sitting at the table behind us, and nobody asked them for autographs. Lawrence looked at us and said, "What's going on here? Who is this kid?"

"Don't you know?" said a woman sitting near him. "That's our boy from Chicago, Stan Mikita."

This proves my point that it's fairly hard for us to get privacy. Sure, it's mighty flattering to be recognized so often and to have fans asking you for autographs, but athletes and their wives are human, too. They want to get away from time to time and have a little privacy just like everybody else.

Perhaps our most comfortable moments away from home are spent with relatives. Every once in a while we visit my sister Irene and her husband Joe Palkovic in Toronto, and we see my Mom and Dad, the ones in St. Catharines, quite often. They also visit us now and then at our house in Elmhurst, Illinois. We have plenty of room, even with three children, because we bought a four-bedroom house a couple of years after we were married.

I guess I've become a family man more and more as I've matured. As for going out, well, we'll still be young enough to do more of that later when the children are older.

16

Back Home Again

I RECOGNIZED the bend in the road by the soccer field and the stream with the moon's light reflected on the waters, and knew I was home again in Sokolce. I couldn't drive fast enough and I was thinking, "What's my father going to say? How is my mother going to act? What is my little sister like?" I hadn't seen her as she had been born a couple of years after I left Czechoslovakia. It was a moment in which you are reaching for something, you are within a hand's grasp of it, you can't wait until you get close enough so you can lunge at it.

It was three o'clock in the morning as we drove into Sokolce and the sound of the car seemed to waken the whole village. All the lights went on and people in their nightwear came out to see what was going on. Dad ran to the door, then realized he had forgotten his glasses and I could hear him yelling, "It's Stano! It's Stano!" My little eight-year-old sister Viera was the first one out of the door. She came leaping out of the house, missed the first two steps, hit the third, and bounced off right into my arms.

We stayed up all night talking.

This was the summer of 1960 and I had been gone twelve years. Although we had exchanged letters and once I had started playing professional hockey I had sent my family money and other things from time to time, it was something else to sit around a table and talk with them face to face, and also to see Viera for the first time.

Mom and Dad both asked me right away, "Are you enjoying life over there? Are you sorry we sent you? Are you angry with us because we gave you up, even if it was to a member of the family?"

I couldn't thank them enough for the opportunity they had given me and I told them so again and again. If it hadn't been for their unselfishness, their *true* love for me, none of the things I was able to accomplish or enjoy would have been possible.

I had always intended to go back to the old country. Not in the way I had dreamed of as a boy, of learning to become an air force pilot so I could fly back, but with the intention of assuring myself everybody was all right and of helping them out as much as I could.

We exchanged letters steadily through the years, but that never satisfied me because I know that people are likely to skip over their troubles when writing so as not to worry you. In the back of my mind there was always the fear that my family in Sokolce was hiding something from me, that something was wrong or someone was sick but they didn't tell me about it so I wouldn't worry. Whenever I opened a letter from home, whether in St. Catharines or later in Chicago, I always had the feeling that this wasn't the whole story. I thought that the only way I could ever have peace of mind was to go back to Czechoslovakia and find out for myself.

I had saved a little money after my first season with the Black Hawks and was able to take my mom and sister Irene from St. Catharines with me so they could visit their relatives, too. I bought a Czech car in Toronto to be delivered in Prague so that we could use it there and then leave it for my brother George.

George met us at the train station in Prague. He looked just as I visualized him. He's about my size, pretty much the same build, so my clothes fit him perfectly and I was able to leave them when we returned to Canada. We picked up the car and drove all night to Sokolce, although we had intended to stop somewhere overnight. But I was too impatient to see the family again to sleep anyway, so we kept driving.

It is a couple of hundred miles from Prague to Sokolce and you can imagine how tiring the drive was, especially for Mother Mikita and Irene, who were in the back seat. The roads were narrow, and often we would have to leave the asphalt highway to take a detour on a dirt road because of construction work. The countryside was beautiful as the road wound along mountainsides and through valleys, but the most beautiful sight of all was that old house in Sokolce.

After the excitement of that first meeting was over, I settled down to a quiet vacation. George and I toured the country in the car, and when we were home I helped out with some of the chores. We went to a dance or two and some family parties and kicked a soccer ball around once in a while. George had a job in the office of a textile factory and played both hockey and soccer on the company teams.

The only time we came in contact with organized sports was in Bratislava, where the national team was in what they called dry training. This is a program of physical conditioning that precedes their actual training on the ice. It's mostly calisthenics and soccer. They asked me if I wanted to work out with them, but being on vacation I politely refused.

I was surprised how much people seemed to know about the National Hockey League, the Black Hawks, and me, especially as I had been with Chicago only one year and hadn't scored that many goals. But I was treated like the prodigal son returning. The sports publications carried stories and scores from the NHL and I had had some mention when I received a few more penalties than was normal.

One of the trip's high spots was seeing the Spartakiade, a huge gymnastics display held every five years in Prague. It was tremendously impressive to sit in a stadium holding a quarter of a million and watch 28,000 people performing calisthenics and ballet-like movements at one time on the field. I wanted to take Jill to see it in 1965, the next time it was held, but we couldn't make it then. In 1960 I thought I'd be back for another visit before seven years passed, but it didn't turn out that way.

Irene, Mother Mikita, and I left to return to St. Catharines in August. Before we went I remember Mother Gvoth asking me if I had met any special girl and if I was thinking of getting married.

"I think I've got a few more years to go before I do that," I said, not knowing it was only three.

"Well, just make sure you love her and that she loves you," said Mother Gvoth. "Don't let anybody talk you into marrying someone you're not sure of loving or let them talk you out of marrying someone you think is right for you."

I know I followed that advice.

After Jill and I were married we talked once in a while about going to Czechoslovakia for a visit, but then Meg was born and later Scott and a real opportunity didn't come until 1967 when the National Film Board in Canada approached me. They were making a TV documentary to be called "Twenty-four

Hours in Czechoslovakia." I was one of three people around whom the film was built, the others being a young girl and an older man. I was offered a small fee plus my expenses for the two weeks it would take to shoot the film. The fee would help pay for Jill and Meg to come along with me, so I accepted.

Jill looked forward to making the trip, but not really with Meg, who was only three; and there was no question of taking Scott, who was just over a year old. But she thought about it and decided it was only right to let Mother Gvoth see Meg because nobody knew when another chance would come, even though relations with the Communist-controlled countries were not strained at the time.

We flew from Chicago to Paris, where incidentally we couldn't get French toast at the airport, then on to Prague, where this time we got a royal welcome. As we got off the plane a young woman greeted us with a loaf of bread in one hand and a dish of salt in the other. It's traditional to greet visitors in this way and I had to cut a wedge of bread myself and put some salt on it, then eat it. I started to eat the bread and it was near disaster. I not only put too much salt on it, but the bread was soft as putty and the partial bridgework of three false teeth I have in front stuck to the bread. I started to take the bridge out of my mouth completely but caught myself in time, and chewed the bread until I got it down. The photographers got some great shots of me with my teeth stuck in the bread—"suave Stosh" they call me.

It was a large delegation that met us at the airport. There were the Film Board people and many Czech sports and news reporters. In the seven years between 1960 and 1967 I had received a lot of publicity in the Czechoslovakian sports magazines and newspapers, and hockey was now so popular in the country that people were eager to read all they could about the Black Hawks and the NHL in general. I had to hold two press conferences, one at the airport and then later at the hotel.

"How long do you think it will be before you play our national team or the Russian team?" was one of the questions.

"I don't know," was all I could say. "It's not up to me."

The reporters knew I had led the NHL in scoring that season so one asked, "How well do you think you'd do if you played here? Would you want to play for our team?"

"I don't think you could afford me," I kidded.

Many other questions came along and I answered them as

Back Home Again

best as I could. I could speak Slovak well, although not as fluently as I would have liked.

The next day we started filming, spending two days in Prague, just walking around sight-seeing, talking to people in the streets, looking in store windows. We enjoyed talking with people who gathered around to watch us. I wore Bermuda shorts now and then, and at that time nobody did there, so I guess they thought I was a little crazy. I could hear some people asking, "Who's that? What's going on?" Somebody would tell them and they'd say, "Oh yes, he's that young American, but somebody should give him money to buy regular pants."

Before we left Prague I sent a telegram to my family in Sokolce, telling them we would be there in about a week. That was the plan, to film at various places along the way, then to spend more time in the town where I had lived as a boy.

Our next stop after Prague was Gottvaldov, where the Czech national hockey team was training. I had met some of the players in Canada while they were visiting various teams on government tours, and was anxious to see some of the others. One of them was Ludo (Louie) Bukac, who had been at the Boston Bruins' training camp one year, and later became coach of the Prague Sparta Club. I spotted about three I thought could play in the NHL. One was the goaltender, Vlado Dzurilla, who later beat the Russian team twice in 1969, touching off patriotic demonstrations in Prague.

At this time, the team was in its third or fourth day of skating, and I was asked if I wanted to get on the ice. I wasn't in condition, but I skated a couple of hours' scrimmage anyway.

A couple of things struck me about the way they play, particularly how high they carry their sticks. They think our game is rough, but while we normally carry the sticks below the shoulder, they carry them much higher and penalties aren't called for high-sticking because of this. They also skate better laterally than we do. One other major difference is that instead of going for a skate (remaining in motion when they lose the puck or have a pass intercepted) they stop and then come back with their check or go in whatever direction they're supposed to. As for the actual speed skating, up and down the ice, I don't know whether they or we, in general, are faster, but there's no doubt they are better conditioned. They train eleven and a half months of the year, while we take off four months in the spring and summer.

There's no doubt they'd like to have a whack at us because a lot of questions pointed in that direction.

"How well do you think we'd do against your club or against Montreal?" they kept asking me. "Do you think we'd have a chance?"

"I think we'd whip you, but I don't know how badly," I said, truthfully. "You might even beat us one game or two games of a seven-game series. And a lot would depend on who played for us and what players you used. There's no way to tell other than in an actual game. Drop the puck and let's go, that would be the only way to find out."

There were a lot of good, knowledgeable hockey questions, too, and I enjoyed talking with so many people who were truly interested in the game.

From Gottvaldov we went to Bratislava, which was the high spot of the trip for Meg because we took her to an amusement park. I'll bet she still relishes that experience because the cameras were grinding and she got plenty of rides to be sure of good film footage. We even thought about taking a hydrofoil down to Vienna, an hour's ride down the Danube, but didn't have time.

We traveled in style. The Film Board provided us with a big Russian-built car and a chauffeur, a Mr. Vesely, who was the life of the party. Vesely means happy in Czech and he was that exactly, a happy-go-lucky guy who couldn't do enough for us.

Liptovsky Mikulas, a town not far from Sokolce, was our next stop, and I had thought since we were so close we would go into our village. But it was getting too dark to film so we had to hold up until the next morning. We already had seen Mother Gvoth, Viera, and my brother George and his wife Ludka and daughter Dana, who is a year younger than Meg. They had spent two or three days with us, then returned home. Now they came up with us into the mountains, and we were able to visit a little more after we finished filming around Sokolce.

My brother even got me into a hockey game. A steel factory in Kosice (where Elmer Vasko's parents were from) approached me through George and asked me to play for their team in an exhibition game against a group from a higher division.

"I haven't been skating regularly for three months," I said. "I'm really out of shape."

"That's all right," was the reply. "You could really help us. We're trying to raise money for uniforms and having you with us should help sell a lot of tickets."

Well, I owe a lot to hockey and if I can repay it in some way I'm always glad to do so. And sports—like music and other arts—seem to link people closer together, regardless of their form of government. Besides, it seemed like it might be a lot of fun, so I agreed to play for them. They were so glad they even picked up the bill for our stay in the mountains and presented us all with fine sheepskin-lined suede coats—a hard-to-get luxury over there.

The game was to be played the day before we were to leave the country. We got to Kosice the day before and I worked out two to three hours with the team. The next night the rink, which seated about six thousand people, was jammed to the rafters. (Jockey Fleming, the Montreal scalper, would have made a killing.) I had to get about fifty tickets for relatives who lived nearby and wanted to attend.

It turned out to be a lot of fun. We won 9-1 and I had four goals and an assist, but what I remember most about the game was catching one six-foot kid coming out of the end zone with his head down. He was passing the puck and just let it go when I came and instinctively hit him with a hip check and sent him flying. I didn't know for a moment whether to start laughing or apologizing because what he had done was a cardinal sin, but I went and helped him up and said I was sorry.

That was the end of a wonderful trip, as we left from Kosice to Prague, then started home. In a way, it was sad because we would never see Sokolce again. It lies in a natural valley and one end of it is being dammed up to form a huge water reservoir that will cover the village. I guess that's progress.

Still, there's a lot of tradition left, over there. There was Roznov, a little town that was celebrating its seven-hundredth anniversary. Imagine that—Canada celebrated its hundredth anniversary in 1967 and the United States will celebrate its two-hundredth in 1976. I was at Roznov the day they celebrated with a small parade and was asked to make a speech in Slovak. They also gave me a commemorative medallion—part gold, part bronze—a fine memento.

I get a lot of fan mail, pictures, postcards, emblems, and clippings of stories, from Czechoslovakia every year. It's heartwarming to know that hockey is a great sport there as it is here and that people think enough of an athlete to want to send him these things.

From Prague we flew to Zurich and then on to Geneva and it's funny how it can be the little things you miss most. The first thing we did at the airport in Zurich was order hamburgers and a Coca-Cola, which Meg and Jill were dying for because they weren't able to get them in Czechoslovakia. And this was at nine o'clock in the morning!

The scenery in Switzerland is comparable to the Tatro Mountains in Slovakia, and Jill and I promised ourselves we'd come back some day and spend a couple of weeks visiting the country.

It was a wonderful trip, and we have a copy of the film that was shown the next year on Canadian TV. It made a fine keepsake and every time we watch it it renews pleasant memories of the country and the fine people.

That trip led to Mother Gvoth and Viera visiting us in Elmhurst in 1968—a much longer visit than they counted on. Viera was studying English in high school in Czechoslovakia and I thought it might be a good chance for her to improve her skill if she came to North America for a few months, and maybe I wanted to show Mother Gvoth how we lived in the U.S. I arranged a two-month visa for them and they arrived in Chicago on July 7, 1968.

Mother Gvoth and Meg and Scott got along wonderfully well. They couldn't understand each other's language but they seemed to sense the meaning. Meg would rattle something off in English and Mom would rattle off a reply in Slovak and the next thing you knew they would both be shaking heads and laughing, getting along fine, although neither one knew what the other was saying.

They stayed with us about a month, then went up to St. Catharines to visit the Mikitas. They had just returned to Chicago when we got the news the Russians had invaded Czechoslovakia. This was August 20 and they were supposed to leave August 23. They didn't know what to do, and finally I stepped in.

"Look, you're not going back until things clear up over there," I said. "We'll see what happens and I'm sure we'll be hearing from George."

As it turned out, I didn't hear from my brother for a month,

Back Home Again / 141

although he was all right, and in the meantime I got Mother Gvoth and Viera an extension of their visa through 1969. My Dad Mikita suggested they come up to St. Catharines and stay with him.

"They can come up here and live with me in St. Catharines until all this blows over," he said. "Viera can go to school here and, who knows, they may want to stay here the rest of their lives."

Mother Gvoth wasn't too happy about this and it took quite a bit of persuading for her to go along. You could see she wasn't happy because this wasn't her homeland and at fifty-five years of age she wasn't ready to start life anew and learn a new language. She had come over mainly to see how we lived and she saw I was doing all right, that she wouldn't have to worry about me any more as a mother always does. She said she still could help my brother—who by this time had a second child, a son Ivan—by looking after the kids while George and his wife worked. Then, too, we all hoped nothing would happen to George and his family if it appeared my mom and sister were seeking political asylum. Viera, of course, didn't say anything because she would do whatever her mother wished. I finally persuaded them to stay until at least the time school was out in 1969.

Viera was eighteen when she arrived and she enjoyed everything, as a young girl will—anything new and different. She didn't pick up more of the language as quickly as I thought she would, chiefly because she was afraid to make mistakes. But after she started school at St. Catharines it seemed to come much better and she could converse in it very well after about five or six months.

Viera met a Czech girl on a visit to us, a good friend of Jill's parents, and they went downtown to look at the sights of Chicago. When Viera came back she said the thing that impressed her most was Buckingham Fountain, which she thought was fantastic with all the colored lights playing on it at night. Isn't that typical? I'd lived in Chicago ten years and had never seen Buckingham Fountain.

It's true there are many wonderful things to see on a trip abroad, but sometimes there are many things near at hand that are equally worth looking at and enjoying. In the future, I plan to do both.

17

It's Worth Trying

IT'S BAFFLING how many "experts" laugh off anything new or different, and almost ridicule anyone willing to try it. Hockey players are the same as other people in that respect and I've always wondered why more of us don't stop and examine any new piece of equipment or variation of an old one with just two questions in mind: Is this practical? Can it help me? If you start with those basic questions, you can eliminate all the useless frills and junk and come down to maybe one or two things that could help your game or keep you playing longer. Both are bound to put money in your pocket.

I don't claim to be another Thomas Edison in that I've ever really invented anything, but I always have tried to improve available equipment so it would be more useful to me; and if in the process other players have benefited, well and good. I don't know that there's a piece of equipment that I haven't tried to modify in some way to suit my own needs, but the two things that I worked with the most during my first ten years in the league were the hockey stick and the helmet. In both cases, my immediate aim was to help myself—first to get the best possible tool with which to handle and shoot the puck, second to develop the finest and lightest protection for the most vital part of my body. That I've been able to help others in helping myself makes it just that much more satisfying.

It may be that I've had been more cursed than blessed for my part in developing the curved hockey stick, but that's only natural. You can't expect goaltenders to be happy about anything that makes their job—already the toughest in sports—more difficult. And if you examine the sources of criticism of the bent blade you'll find most of it comes from goaltenders. After all, they're the ones who fish the puck out of the net. I don't ever recall hearing of a thirty-five-, or forty- or fifty-goal scorer complaining about the curved stick.

It's Worth Trying

I happened on the curved stick by accident. Sometime during the 1960-61 season I was practicing and a stick cracked vertically in the blade without the end breaking off completely. I took a couple of shots with it and the puck seemed to jump, even with the wrist shot I was using. Bobby Hull noticed me fooling around and we talked about it after practice.

We decided to try and bend the blades by putting them under a door and using leverage. We broke a good many sticks, but learned to do the bending gradually. We even tried running hot water over the blades, but had to abandon that because they became water-logged and too heavy to use after the protective plastic coating was removed while shaving them down. Still, we made do with bending them on our own until we got a manufacturer to make them to our specifications.

Of course, we weren't the first to use a bent stick. Apparently Andy Bathgate, who played for many years with the New York Rangers and other teams, also had tried one. But it's safe to say that Bobby and I touched off the interest that led to a lot of other players adopting a curved blade during the next few seasons. We also touched off many newspaper and magazine stories on the "banana blade" and its advantages and disadvantages. One point overlooked in most of these articles was that the curved shape of the blade was continually changing, that what they were criticizing as a disadvantage had been removed through experimentation and modification.

Development of the stick was a continuing thing with me. I made some change almost every season. At first the blade was bent like a banana, curved from the heel to the toe. With it I couldn't control the puck easily on the backhand. It occurred to me to keep the blade straight halfway from the heel to the toe, then start the curvature, but that didn't give me quite the control I wanted. Soon I kept the blade straight two-thirds of the way from the heel to the toe and started the curve at that point, producing almost a hook the last one-third of the way to the tip.

A great advantage of the bent blade from my standpoint was that while skating I could shoot off either foot. I could keep skating without hesitating to raise the back leg and fire the puck. I got a better shot while in motion. And as I got closer to the goaltender with a defenseman trying to ride me out of the play or backing in, I could pull the puck towards me a little bit and shoot past his feet all in the same motion, almost creating a screen shot. These were two of the biggest advantages.

The effect of the curved stick on the puck was more apparent to the goaltenders than to me. But they say the puck had a tendency to take off, rise more than it did with a straight stick —that it dipped, hopped, and curved coming in, making it more difficult for them to judge the flight of the puck.

A frequent criticism was that the curved stick made the art of stick-handling obsolete. Actually, I found it easier to handle the puck with the new stick. Stick-handling is the art of controlling the puck, and since 85% of it is done on the forehand, the hook of the stick makes it easier. I can go up and down the lineups of every hockey team and pick out the players who are considered stick-handlers. Every one of them tries to beat his opposition on his forehand. He may make a move, a fake to the backhand, but when he brings the puck back it's always to his forehand. The bent blade cradles the puck on the same principle as the jai alai stick or a lacrosse stick cradles the balls used in those games.

Taking a pass on the forehand is also easier even if the puck bounces away a little bit. You can still grab it because of the hook, and the puck seems to stick to it better. On the backhand, though, it's tougher to take a pass, but it can be done if you have the right kind of curved blade and know how to use it. The trick is to get the pass on the straight part of the blade and the puck will lie dead rather than bounce away as it would if it hit the curved part. It's a matter of having the right stick and learning how to use it.

It's the same thing with passing. You can do it on the backhand if you move the puck off the flat part near the heel. On the forehand you do it just the opposite, off the hook near the toe. The problem comes when you're using a banana blade, one with a curve all the way from heel to toe.

I'll admit the backhand shot has pretty well gone out of the game. In recent years a couple of the best at using it were Jean Beliveau of Montreal and Jean Ratelle of New York. Beliveau used a straight stick, but Ratelle used a slight curve. The curved stick has been blamed for almost eliminating the backhand shot, but I think other changes in the game have had as much to do with it. The same changes that have almost eliminated the art of passing, such as the tactic of just dumping the puck in the other team's end and chasing it rather than working it in.

It's Worth Trying / 145

Perhaps the curved stick has encouraged greater use of the slap shot. I don't know. Since Boom Boom Geoffrion perfected the slap shot it has become accepted as a pretty good offensive weapon. He scored fifty goals with it, and then Bobby Hull came along and scored even more goals, so that everybody else tried it. And because Bobby used both the slap shot and the curved stick it might have seemed to people that the two went together.

It has been said that scoring went up with the curved stick, but that might have been just a coincidence with the other changes in the game that opened it up. For one thing, the players of today are a lot bigger and stronger on the average than they were twenty years ago and can shoot the puck harder. Combine that with the popularity of the slap shot and you've got the puck traveling with greater force, and it's hard for the goaltender to tell where the puck is going, just as the shooters aren't sure about the exact direction of their shots—regardless of whether it's a straight or a curved blade. As a result, the goaltenders sort of pull up, not wanting to get hit in the head. My point is that maybe they're more afraid of the slap shot itself, not of the sticks. But it may seem a lot easier to blame the curved stick and to criticize the guys who are using it.

I'm not saying that every player can or should use a curved stick. As a matter of fact youngsters new to the game would be better off learning the fundamentals of stick-handling with a straight blade and work up to the curved stick. Among the experienced players there might be some who can't adjust to using a curved stick. Jean Beliveau, I'm told, tried it but didn't like it, though I don't know the length of his trial. Maybe he didn't give it a chance. After eight years of using the curved blade I was still learning new ways of handling the stick; I could do certain things in 1969 I couldn't do two years earlier. For example, it was tougher to take a face-off and get the puck back with the curved stick, so I had to figure out new ways to do it. I got a split-second jump on my opponent and tried to outguess the referee as to exactly when he was dropping the puck. I kept fooling with the stick, getting more curve, less curve within the legal limits, and also varying the point between the heel and toe at which the curvature started.

(The NHL rule on sticks reads in part: "The curvature of the blade of the stick shall be restricted in such a way that the distance of a perpendicular line measured from a straight line drawn between the heel and end of the blade to the point of maximum curvature shall not exceed one and one-half inches.")

When Bobby and I first started using the curved sticks people sort of looked on us as oddballs—"What the hell is that? Are you going to try and shoot the puck around corners?" There wasn't much criticism though when things were going well, when the sticks seemed to be working for us.

The second-guessing came when things weren't going well. Let's face it, everybody gets into a slump, if that's the word. Anyway, that's the term used when you're having bad luck or not playing well enough. But if we went into a slump people would get on our backs. It's the curved stick, they'd say, get rid of it and you'll be playing better and scoring more goals. Then a game would come along in which you'd break out with two or three goals and suddenly the sticks would be all right.

This does bring up a point about the changing of rules pertaining to equipment specifications in all levels of organized hockey. Of course, I realize that you can't have people making up their own rules or designing equipment every which way without some basic guidelines. Otherwise you might just wind up with hockey stick blades two feet long, with fish nets along the blade to scoop up the puck and hold it all night. But I feel generally there's an attitude that because a rule is on the books, it isn't meant to be adapted or changed ever, that it's the very best possible solution.

I guess I feel that there should be more open discussion, with adequate presentations by every segment of those connected with a sport—including the widest cross-section of athletes who are most affected by rule changes or lack of changes. The way things are now, it's easy to reach an arbitrary decision based on the personal opinions of a few influential people —in practically any sport you can think of, at almost any level of play from amateur to professional.

For instance, it's just possible curved sticks might be outlawed entirely under this kind of setup because a few of the right people had their minds made up beforehand without a thorough investigation of all the facts and fair consideration of all opinions. The summary of the minutes of such a policy meeting might read: Curved blades are dangerous and they're no good and we didn't have them before and don't want them now or ever.

It's Worth Trying / 147

As I think back, I realize that I almost gave up the curved stick once or twice. After someone starts harping on you about a certain thing you begin thinking about it, begin second-guessing yourself. Once you start doing that you're messed up completely. But I resisted the temptation. I told myself that I had done well with the curved stick, that things just weren't breaking for me at the moment, that the puck wasn't going in, that's all, and that it would start again one of these days if I kept working. And it did.

This business of blaming equipment or other foolish things for a player's shortcomings reminds me of a story about J.C. Tremblay, the great Montreal defenseman. Tremblay wore long sideburns and also a helmet. Some people don't like sideburns, others don't like helmets on hockey players. Tremblay happened to get into a slump and every critic had his own diagnosis. One even wrote seriously that Tremblay wasn't playing well because he had long sideburns, apparently that it was a sign of being dissipated or against some unwritten law. Another wrote that the helmet was making J.C. play poorly. Tremblay had an answer for both of them.

"I play this way whether I have sideburns or not or whether I wear a helmet or not," said Tremblay. "Sometimes things go for you, sometimes they don't. But it's J.C. playing the game, it's not the helmet and it's not the sideburns."

This is very true. Too many people try to find an alibi by pinning the blame on a piece of equipment such as skates, sticks or helmets, or something as far out as hair, but the truth is it's mostly the man inside a uniform that's to blame if things aren't going right.

Even Coach Billy Reay forgot this once in a while. I remember his coming up to me once and asking, "Do you really have to use that curved stick?" And another time, "Do you really have to wear a helmet?" I reminded him that I hadn't done too badly with the stick and, for that matter, with the helmet. Also, that the helmet covered a vital part of my body important to my family—and to me.

I first wore a helmet for any length of time after I took a two-handed whack with a stick on the forehead from Kent Douglas in Toronto in a game during the 1965-66 season. It took fourteen stitches to close the wound, which was just inside the hairline, not long—but deep. Fortunately, that's the thickest part of the skull so the damage wasn't great, but I had a heck of a headache. I put a helmet on the next game and kept it on the rest of the season until the very last game of the playoffs.

That helmet, uncomfortable as it was, saved me from several injuries, I'm sure. At that time Gilles Marotte—later with the Hawks—was still with Boston; and I can remember his getting me in a corner and hitting me from behind so that the front of my head struck a metal support between two panes of the protective glass around the rink. If I hadn't had the helmet I'm sure I would have suffered at least a deep cut, if not a more serious injury. Marotte also ran at me from the front a couple of times and knocked me to the ice. Once the back of my head struck the ice, and I'm sure the helmet again saved me from a possible concussion.

But the helmet was unsatisfactory. For one thing I didn't feel really protected, it seemed so flimsy. And it was much too hot and uncomfortable, often slipping or sliding around when I moved my head. It fit right next to my head, touching every part of it, and if I forced a small size on for a snug fit that wouldn't move around, I'd get a headache and really sweat. If it felt fairly comfortable to begin with, it would eventually flop around. The thing was lined with a coarse styrofoam which would soften after two periods as I sweated into it, but would harden again between games and present the same breaking-in problem the next time out. It was quite light, a thin plastic—maybe too light to be safe under a severe test—but as I wasn't used to having something on my head when playing, it was a nuisance and felt heavy anyhow.

I resolved the next season to keep looking for a satisfactory helmet, meanwhile continuing to play without one, although I tried several different available types in practice. My new business advisor, Al Macejak, and I had talked about producing a suitable helmet when we first associated in the summer of 1967, and we already were in contact with George Dan, an imaginative sporting goods design engineer who had extensive experience with football helmets, but things were still in the planning stages.

The next time I wore a helmet for any length of time was after I had my ear nearly cut off by a puck on December 16, 1967. Then in mid-January of '68, Bill Masterton of the Minnesota North Stars died as a direct result of hitting the back of his head on the ice after being bodychecked during a game.

It's Worth Trying / 149

That made a lot of players stop and think, and my earlier thoughts about designing my own helmet became a lot more urgent.

When the writers came and asked if I was going to wear a helmet, I didn't hesitate. "Yes, I am," I said. "This is the thing that has hit the closest to home as far as I'm concerned because Masterton was an NHL player, a damn good one, and he had a family, a wife and two kids at home. All of a sudden they're left with $50,000. Well, money can't replace him at home with those kids and that wife."

I knew that if something could happen once it could happen twice. If a helmet could save my life I was going to wear one from then on. As dissatisfied as I was with those available, I put one on the next game and kept wearing it the rest of the season.

Some other NHL players also put on helmets and wore them for a while but discarded them after a few games, mostly because they were uncomfortable and the men just couldn't get used to them. On our team, Doug Mohns and Pierre Pilote continued to wear them, as I did.

In the summer of 1968, I spent some money and began producing prototypes of my new helmet. I told my engineer associate what I wanted: a webbed suspension system that would keep the shell away from my head yet firmly seated so it couldn't wiggle around; light weight; lots of ventilation; as much protection as possible; and even something that would look good when I wore it. He went to the drawing-board and we came up with a shell that conformed more to the head than a football helmet does, so it wouldn't stick out as far or ride as high on the head. We made other modifications in order to protect the neck area and not block vision in any direction, also continually cutting the weight down and improving the suspension and adding some padded parts until we got just what I wanted.

I started wearing the new helmet in training camp in September, 1968, and it proved a great improvement over anything I had worn before. We kept making minor modifications as the season went along, but this was the only helmet that I wore through the entire 1968-69 season. I became so used to wearing and playing with it, that even if I was without it just for scrimmage, I didn't feel right.

It was rather surprising how much unsolicited interest my

new helmet generated—from NHL players and from players and coaches from the PeeWee level up to other pro leagues. It became a problem, as each helmet was made almost entirely by hand and we weren't set up to fit players properly. But we did our best to supply at least one helmet to each of the dozens of NHL players who contacted me. Since it suited me and others in the NHL, some of whom had never worn a helmet before, I knew we were on the right track and I went ahead and filed patent applications in both the U.S. and Canada.

My new helmet has already saved me from a number of cuts and minor injuries, and it may have saved my life or certainly prevented a crippling injury. The instance I'm referring to happened in a Montreal game when I slammed head-on into the metal goal post after scoring. I was moving toward the net at a pretty good pace, but slowed myself down a bit with a lateral motion. As I rammed the puck into the net, I was both sliding and falling down and realized there was no way to avoid a collision, so I consciously turned my head so that the top of the helmet would meet the post. The suspension cushioned the blow and I didn't feel it on top of my head. Without my helmet, I'm sure my skull would have been cracked open or my neck would have taken most of the blow, probably resulting in a broken neck rather than the slight sore neck I had the following morning. I just got up and walked away from the play.

People have often asked me why all the players didn't wear helmets. It may seem silly but I think most of them were worried about their courage being questioned, and there was also a long tradition of not wearing helmets, mostly promoted by the coaches and owners, in my opinion. Some coaches had the attitude, "I didn't wear one when I played, and now that I'm coaching I don't want my players to wear one." Then, wearing a helmet would be a change from what one is used to, and there's a psychological resistance to any change.

I'm positive that someday all NHL players will wear helmets, possibly of their own accord, as younger players who have been wearing helmets from the beginning move up into the NHL. Right now, I think the quickest and only sure way to make the pros wear helmets is to make it mandatory, although it would be better if players acted voluntarily. I really don't know why the league didn't do so after Masterton was killed. Maybe some of the general managers and coaches were afraid that if a man who scored forty goals the year before without a helmet dropped to nineteen or twenty the next season, he would blame the helmet for having caused his poor year.

There was also the argument that if the fellows wore helmets there would be an increase in stick swinging and high sticking, everybody would be aiming for the head figuring it was protected. If that's so, then the way to stop it would be some swift action in dealing out stiff fines or to set an example by suspending players for a few games. Another excuse was that helmets would make it harder for the fans to identify the players. That didn't make any sense either because any hockey helmet doesn't sit as far in front as a football helmet and there's normally no face guard to block the view. Football fans don't enjoy that game any less. In fact, the hard-shell helmet opened up football more, made it even more exciting. I think the same will be true of hockey, only more so.

Even without realizing it, I'm sure most NHL players play a more cautious style to compensate for not having some head protection. Once a player accepts the idea of wearing a helmet and gets used to it on his head, I think he'll skate a little harder and go all out a bit oftener because he knows he's protected when he takes chances.

Some knowledgeable hockey people have also suggested that fans like the idea of danger associated with the sport, that they get a kick out of blood and all that. Apparently, these hockey experts feel the other protective padding worn is all right but that the head should remain extra vulnerable, so long as it's someone else's head. Well, maybe all humans have some dark, secret urge to see an injury happening to someone else, but I'd say the average fan comes to a stadium expecting his money's worth in fast, hard action, with the excitement coming from the natural speed and pace of the game and from winning or just from his team scoring, or seeing some unbelievable play.

There is one way helmets might become universal fairly fast, without making them mandatory. If every superstar in the league could be persuaded to wear one, it would set a great example. If men like Gordie Howe, Jean Beliveau, and Bobby Hull wore them—or say the entire All-Star team wore them—the others would do likewise.

I found this out early: set an example, and there are plenty who follow suit if it's a good idea. In this regard, I wonder how many NHL players would ever allow their sons to play in a hockey game without wearing a helmet. Howe's youngsters, Marty and Mark, both wear helmets, and three of Bobby Hull's boys, Bobby Jr., Blake, and Brett, never go on the ice without them. You can't draw the line as a person grows up because the head certainly doesn't become harder or the danger any less. Maybe an adult does know how to skate better and handle himself on the ice because of greater experience, but then he also moves faster and weighs more and comes up against men at his own level of skill, so the chances of injury may be greater.

When it comes to trying new things, using new equipment, or trying different ways of doing something, I think it pays to experiment and keep an open mind. And I'd rather be the first guy than the last in this regard, too.

18

Me a Vice-President?

LIKE MOST KIDS, it took me a while to really start thinking about the future, what I would do when my hockey career ended. When you're twenty and single you really don't worry too much about things like that; but a few years later, when you have a wife and growing family and time slips by faster, you begin to seriously consider what you're going to do if you're injured, or your career is cut short.

Most of us hockey players lack a complete formal education partly because of the way hockey is structured in Canada, although more and more are coming into the league out of college now, especially with hockey taking hold in the U.S. schools. But generally, most of us didn't finish high school, we had no profession or trade to fall back on if our careers ended. We kidded a lot about always being able to go out and dig ditches for a living, but we realized there was no hope of maintaining our standard of living unless we made a more realistic provision for the future.

I had heard of many athletes who had great opportunities but didn't take advantage of them. I also realized that there were a lot of hockey players who didn't have the chance to capitalize on their names that I had, because of all the publicity I received. I said to myself, "I've got the exposure and this opportunity now. If I can make use of it, fine. If I don't it's nobody's fault but my own."

So a few years ago, I set out to make the best of it, and I took a step more and more professional athletes are now doing. I became associated with someone who had the background and time to investigate the many business offers that were around and even to drum up some endorsements for me —probably not swimsuits, though. Through Al Macejak—who was a merchandising man in the advertising business—I entered into some long-range deals, and Al now works for me together with the organization run by Mark McCormack.

I suppose I let myself in for a little kidding when I took the title of vice-president in 1969 with Christian Bros., Inc., a then small but good hockey stick manufacturing firm in Warroad, Minnesota, near the Canadian border. The title was somewhat misleading. Actually it would have been more appropriate to call me Director of Product Development, because that's what my duties involved. Still, imagine, an under-thirty little DP flashing a fancy business card that announced "Vice-President"!

My attempts to start a career outside of hockey weren't that fancy at the beginning. While negotiating on my own, I tried about three sales jobs before I realized that I was no salesman. One summer, for a month, I took a crack at selling liquor on the road for a distributing firm owned by Mr. Norris and Mr. Wirtz. I discovered you had to drink with the bartenders and the cocktail lounge owners to be a good fellow and I couldn't be quite that friendly since I seldom touch hard liquor. Then I tried selling insurance. I even took a course in insurance and learned what a wonderful thing it was, but I just wasn't the kind of person to do that type of persistent contacting and selling, letting all the "no's" spur me on harder. My third attempt in the field of selling was for a company manufacturing pressed-board backs for TV sets, and it ended the same way.

But like most experiences these didn't go to waste. I had learned what I was best suited for and what I wasn't. I had also discovered that my time alone wasn't the most valuable thing I had to offer. My name and reputation and what I knew about hockey had a far greater value. And I learned something about business, although I still wasn't prepared for the experience I had with Stan Mikita's Village Inn. This was a restaurant I became associated with in Oak Brook Shopping Center, west of Chicago, not far from my home in Elmhurst.

Through one of Jill's friends, I was in touch with a family in the restaurant business, and after some basic investigation, we reached an agreement. My name would be used with the restaurant although it would be operated by one of the family members who knew the restaurant business. After opening on June 13, 1968, it proved very successful and business volume was tremendous.

Me a Vice-President? / 155

I tried to get over to the restaurant as much as possible, although it was difficult during the hockey season. I realized that a lot of people came the first time in hopes that I would be there so they could meet me, shake hands or get an autograph or picture, and I made it a point to drop by as often as I could during the peak lunch and dinner periods. However, if they liked the food and service, they'd be back.

From the first, I expected to learn as much about the restaurant business as I could. I had always wanted to know what a restaurant was really like, what the people did behind the scenes. I planned to learn first hand what pleased the customers, what made them unhappy. And since my name was associated with the business, I wanted to be fully aware of how things were going. My restaurant associate and I sat down from time to time and discussed how we might improve the quality of the food or the service. But it wasn't my role to actually manage the operation and I relied on my associate.

This was a mistake! I had been receiving monthly figures which showed the venture was doing quite well and during our conferences, my associate assured me that things couldn't be better.

On July 21, 1969, after more than a year of operation, I received a phone call at home from this associate. He said, "I'm going broke"—just like that! And he refused to discuss it or give any explanation by phone. This was Monday and since I had to pick up my children, who were with their grandmother at a summer cottage for the weekend, we set up a meeting for Wednesday. Shortly before this meeting, I got another phone call at home and was told that the employees' keys had been taken away and the door locks were being replaced. The restaurant was closed and out of business—with no warning of any kind to me or the employees.

I was stunned! I thought first of the employees and the suppliers. I wondered what the public would think. How could this possibly happen? But it had and there was nothing I could do about it by the terms of my contract with the owner, since he was responsible for running things. It took several days before I even noticed my family, I was so shocked and upset. One day, by all appearances and volume, I was associated with a highly successful business. The next day it was suddenly over and I was just another person among the creditors. All I could do was make every effort to see that people were paid.

It's not for me to go into the legal or moral aspects of the situation here. I doubt that we'll ever be able to piece together the full story, but I'll say that it became more apparent than ever before that a man's honesty and reputation are his most valuable possessions. I would rather be broke than lose them.

I had just as great an interest in the quickly expanding hockey equipment business. This has had a tremendous growth in recent years, yet I think it's still just starting. The possibilities are excellent because kids are taking up hockey all over the United States in numbers that would have been unbelievable just a few years ago. The expansion of the NHL to twelve teams and the games on TV have created a great surge of interest among youngsters in learning and playing the game. I know that when I first came to the Chicago area in 1959 kids' leagues were almost unheard of and there were very few artificial-ice rinks. Ten years later, many thousands of youngsters were playing organized hockey and the number of rinks had risen sharply. Hockey was really taking off.

Naturally, the hockey equipment industry was booming, but it bothered me that a lot of the equipment being sold wasn't as good as it should have been for the money. People nowadays, particularly in the United States, aren't afraid to spend money when it comes to buying protection for their kids, but a lot of the equipment sold was inadequate. I think some manufacturers were stereotyped in their thinking, approaching everything from a price angle only, and a majority of the stuff was designed by people who had never played hockey in their lives. They didn't know where the padding should go or how the thighs or shins should be protected or what sort of protection should be built into the skates. If these companies had asked hockey players they might have learned what to do.

Take the skates. I've told many an equipment supplier that I'd like this or that change made in my skates, and if they had been listening they could have copied the final product and have come out with a fine boot. It wouldn't have cost them any more to manufacture but I think it would have been twice the boot they were selling. The same goes for other pieces of equipment.

I felt a number of manufacturers could do a lot to improve

Me a Vice-President? / 157

the quality of the equipment they were selling, especially the stuff being sold to youngsters. The kids need more built-in protection because they don't know that much about the game and are more liable to be hurt than adults who, generally, know how to improvise in order to correct equipment shortcomings. The kids don't know how to do this. They look at a piece of equipment and are influenced in buying it if they are told an NHL player helped design it or uses something like it. This is especially true in the United States where advertising and endorsements make such a difference in sales.

Of all sports it seemed to me hockey had the greatest potential as far as equipment sales go. I felt that if I could help improve the design with the aid of somebody who could handle the technical aspects it would be an opportunity to benefit the kids and hockey.

This was one of the reasons I became associated with Christian Bros. Over the years I had a lot of trouble getting the quality of sticks I wanted. Out of each batch of a dozen sticks I ordered, I sometimes might get just one that suited me, because there was no consistency. When we were in touch with Bill and Roger Christian—both knowledgeable young men who won fame a few years back when the U.S. Olympic squad took its first hockey gold medal—I was really interested.

Not only were they leading amateur hockey players, they were both wood craftsmen by trade and already had a part-time company set up, manufacturing top-notch hockey sticks which were widely used, principally by teams throughout Minnesota. They were planning to sell some stock in order to expand production facilities right away. We signed a long-range agreement that we would pool our knowledge and I'd advise them on all sticks and help develop other new sticks. Some special models would carry my name and, like all their sticks, stress quality first. I was so sure the venture couldn't miss that I invested some money in the company.

It's a fact that I'm as concerned about my reputation with anyone I associate with as the chance of adding to my income, and I knew there wouldn't be any worries with as fine people as Roger, Bill, and the others helping run the company. I felt my name and hockey know-how would help the company to get going nationally, and I was anxious to work with them because they had a fresh viewpoint, were energetic, and wanted the ideas I could contribute. In the long run, I knew kids would be able to get better equipment for their money, and if a youngster has the right stick it's part of developing him correctly as a hockey player.

The same reasoning applies to other equipment, such as the helmet I had developed. As I said before, we produced them individually at first only to fill requests from fellow NHL players. Knowing they did a better job than anything else I could find, it was the next step to manufacture and distribute them in the United States and Canada. We chose our manufacturer and distributors very carefully—because my name went with the product and I wanted it to be right.

There are other pieces of equipment that I may now just go ahead and modify or design myself with sound engineering help. Then if the equipment does the job for me, I'll patent it and arrange for the manufacturing and distribution. I saw what could happen when I started working on a helmet—mostly just so I could have something that suited me. Most important of all, this way I'll know that if my name is associated with a product it's pretty good and the endorsement isn't just a gimmick.

I remember going to a sports show once and examining some of the hockey equipment that was being exhibited. A lot of it was of poor quality, and I wondered out loud how they could peddle such junk. A salesman told me, "Listen, if you get a piece of garbage and package it properly, dress it up, people are going to buy it because they don't really know that much about it, especially when it's new to them."

As far as I'm concerned that's the next thing to picking pockets. It's not doing hockey on the whole any good either. People deserve their money's worth and should be able to count on the equipment they buy to do the job it's supposed to do.

Through a special corporation I've set up, I now undertake a number of other projects covering a wide area. To give an idea, one of the ventures involves offering color poster caricatures of leading NHL players. This has already proved to be a popular item because there's nothing around like it, and it keeps my artist friend Bob Pelkowski busy.

Working with the right staff, I find business doesn't interfere with my hockey efforts and allows me to be a hockey player first and only incidentally a businessman during the season, although I do keep on top of things.

You could sum up my philosophy by saying that whatever I'm associated with, I want to be a winner, whether it's a hockey team, a restaurant or equipment to keep the game as great as it is.

19

Friends, Fans, and Phonies

YOU MIGHT think that an athlete has to be on guard every moment to protect himself from the phonies who are attracted to him because he's so well known. And it's partly true because you'd be a fool not to realize there are a lot of people who would like to use you or your name to promote some project of their own. Still, it's not all that difficult to separate the real friends from the phonies who show up from time to time.

There are a number of tests to separate friends from phonies, but one of the better ones is to find out if a guy is willing to return a favor for one you've done for him. Phonies are always asking for something, whether it's to get them tickets to a hockey game, to make public appearances for this or that project, or to endorse any number of things. Then, when in return you ask them for a little favor, they usually say, "Gee, Stan, I'd like to do that for you but there's something coming up and I won't be able to get at it." You discover that with them friendship is all one-sided—you give, they take.

Phonies have another trait in common. They're always the first ones to get on your back when things aren't going well, when the team is losing or you're in a slump. They start talking behind your back, and don't always stop there, but let you have it right out in the open. I've even heard people who I thought were friends or, at the least, personal acquaintances, yelling at me in the Stadium if I happened to miss an open net or hit the goal post. "Look at that bum," they'd yell, "he can't even put the puck in the ocean." Sometimes they'd get a little more personal.

Luckily, you can weed out most of these people before they have a chance to take advantage of you. I suppose I've been offered a million opportunities to get involved in this, that, or the other thing. Almost every day somebody would offer me

Friends, Fans, and Phonies

some sort of wonderful deal, whether it was a hot tip on the stock market, a piece of booming business, or a chance to get in on the ground floor of a project to sell hockey sticks in the Congo. Thank you and goodbye was the best way to handle these great opportunities.

Fortunately, most of the people I've gotten to know through hockey were not at all like this. I've made any number of good, honest friendships in and out of the game and I treasure every one of them.

You can't really list people as No. 1, No. 2, No. 3, and so on in order of friendships, but among the players I was closest to were Kenny Wharram, Glenn Hall, Ab McDonald, Eddie Litzenberger, and Doug Mohns. Very often there was also a close relationship among the wives too and we'd go out together or play bridge.

Kenny and I tried to relax together as much as possible, and as I explained before, if the team or our line wasn't going well we would talk things over and see if we could figure something out. Maybe we'd pass it on to the others, too.

Then, we helped each other out, like working on the recreation room at my house in Elmhurst. Without Kenny I don't think I would have accomplished much. He's an expert cabinetmaker, but with me, it's just a case of hitting a nail with a hammer and, as often as not, I'd be more likely to bend the nail or hit my finger.

Naturally, I didn't get to see Glenn Hall as often as I'd have liked after he left the club. Jill and Glenn's wife, Pauline, also had become the best of friends, and as often as we could, we'd try to see them, but it was increasingly difficult with our growing families. Glenn would telephone when he got into Chicago and I'd do the same when I got to St. Louis.

I don't want anyone to think that friendships affect the game on the ice. I don't believe they do, whether the friendships are with your own teammates or men on the other team. It's a team game and we're paid to try and win, so friendship shouldn't affect the play. Yet it can help in an indirect way, one that you can't measure. If there's a feeling of comradeship between the six men on the ice, if they get along well together off the ice, it could be that this would help their play. There's no way to measure this, or even to prove that it exists, but it's reasonable to think it does.

From the start, I also made a lot of friends off the ice, and if I mentioned them all this would look like the Chicago telephone book. There are Irv and Harriet Tiahnybik, whom I met through Eddie Litzenberger. Jill and I often went out with them. I'd do favors for him and he'd do favors for me, which is one of the things I think friendships are for. Irv's dad owned the Leon Sausage Company in Chicago and Irv always had taken an interest in the hockey players. Once a year he'd have a party for the fellows and their wives at their suburban Lincolnwood home. Irv and I had occasion to see each other about once a week, or we might talk something over on the phone two or three times, that's how close we are.

Another friend almost from the start was Mickey Madigan, an insurance man, who introduced me to Jill. There is Ed Staren, in the meat business, Bob Hielscher, another insurance man, and Jay McGreevy, in the kitchen appliance field. And many others.

Most of these fellows I play golf with, which is my favorite way of relaxing. I can't think of a better way to get my mind off a problem than to go out on the golf course, and no sport offers a sharper contrast with hockey. In hockey you need somebody else to help you, you really can't accomplish much by yourself, but in golf you go out there strictly on your own. Either you do it by yourself or you fail. It's a completely different sort of challenge to me, trying to beat par first of all, then trying to beat your opponents.

I started playing golf in St. Catharines, and had a fourteen or fifteen handicap almost from the beginning, then lowered it to a five. But I made one mistake, I didn't take lessons from a professional until after I had been playing more than ten years. It pointed out something to me that we tend to overlook. You can learn more from talking with a professional in a sport than you can from any other source. I think I know a lot about hockey but that doesn't mean I know a lot about golf, certainly nothing to compare with what a pro knows about it. A pro in any sport knows best about his own game and if you want to learn, go to him. That goes for a kid wanting to play hockey or for a hockey player wanting to play a better game of golf.

I'm sure any golfer who reads this will pardon me for mentioning the hole-in-one I shot on August 15, 1958, at St. Catharines Golf Club. It was 145 yards on a par-three hole over a little water. When I swung I thought I had missed the shot as I almost topped the ball and it was a low tee shot. It hit about ten feet in front of the pin, took a single bounce about six feet past the hole and then took the backspin and rolled in. Just like hockey! If it's going to go in, it goes in no matter what you do. I almost had another one playing with Ron Murphy, Bobby Hull and Mickey Madigan—but, as they say, being close counts only in horseshoes.

The year before I was married I lived with Dr. Lou and Marie Seno and their family in Hillside, just east of Elmhurst. I shared a room with their oldest son Steve, and I really enjoyed living with them, particularly since it was a new experience for me to be part of a large family of five boys and a girl. After my first child was born, Doc honored us by becoming Meg's godfather. Dr. Seno also got to know many of the other Hawks in the following years and quite a few lived in apartments he owns. In the summer, he also has some members of the White Sox baseball team staying there. The Senos did everything possible to make a player's stay pleasant and every year they have a party for the families.

After we were married, Jill and I bought the house in Elmhurst and when we first moved in some of the neighbors must have regarded us as a novelty. Naturally, they were curious because I was fairly well known by this time, but once we settled down it got to be a normal, friendly relationship. Emily and Bill Tvarusek even became godparents to our third child, Jane Elizabeth. You couldn't ask for better neighbors than we had.

You also couldn't ask for better fans than we had at the Stadium—that is, most of them. From time to time, it seemed a handful came to disrupt the action by throwing eggs or other debris on the ice. Fans get worked up sometimes and show their displeasure by hurling a program or hat, but when someone goes to the trouble of bringing raw eggs or a bag of metal shavings and keeps tossing those things, they've got to be sick people. It not only delays the game but presents a serious hazard for the skaters on both sides. Some of those objects could knock out an eye, and you could break a leg just by gliding over a small scrap of paper and I think these few nuts were aware of that and even hoped it would happen.

Even off the ice, say at a public place, most fans were well behaved and polite. Normally they just ask for autographs, which you usually don't mind giving. You even get a kick out of it once in a while when they say it's for their kids and you know they want it for themselves. In a way, you're flattered to be recognized and, although it's a bother at times or you need some privacy, this is a part of the life that's expected of you.

I seldom ran into trouble with the fans leaving the rink because most of them understand that you leave the game on the ice. Once in a while there's a smart aleck who throws a dig, usually just to show off to his girl friend that he can belittle you and get away with it. You try to let it go in one ear and out the other and not let yourself get upset.

I never found too much difference in fans in one city from those of another, and most fans, whatever the sport is, will be happy if they have a club that wins at least as many games as it loses, providing that some years you give them a championship. They're there primarily for entertainment. Naturally, they are out to see you win each game and I suppose it would be ideal if every team won all its home games and lost all the games on the road. That way, all the fans leaving the rink or ballpark would be perfectly satisfied.

There've been cases in which the reaction of the fans has made players wish they would be traded. It was quite understandable that Glenn Hall no longer wanted to play in Chicago when it got to the point that the fans would boo him every time he had a bad night, even if it was seldom. They forgot what he had done for the team for a dozen years and that an athlete is human and not a machine. Once the fans get down on a guy they don't let up easily. They did the same thing to Dennis Hull for a while, and to Pierre Pilote, before he was traded to Toronto. In cases like that it might be better for the player and the team if he's traded so he can get a fresh start elsewhere. It's not so much that players can't perform well without fan support, but mostly that they can do without the booing. If they're young it saps their confidence, too.

The first time I actually heard myself booed on home ice was that night in March, 1969, when the goal announced as having been scored by our rookie defenseman Ray McKay was corrected and credited to me. It shook me at first to hear the boos, but on second thought I could understand the fans' reaction. They thought it was the kid's first goal in the league, that he had been trying hard and playing well and that I

Friends, Fans, and Phonies / 165

hadn't, and the team was buried in last place. Of course, everybody is entitled to his opinion but when you tie your own record of ninety-seven points in a season it seems odd to say you haven't been playing as well as in the past. Maybe some people thought I had been loafing, too. Well, it appears to me that when a player in any sport is a young rookie, he may run around a bit more to make up for what he lacks in experience or polish. As he gets a few years of pro play under his belt, his skill usually increases and he knows how to meet a situation better. This doesn't mean he tries any the less or loafs.

Watch the really good veterans in any sport. They produce results and still give it all they've got but it looks different—maybe they make things look easy, whereas they might have expended more energy and gone through wasted motions in rookie years. I think I still play just as hard as I ever did, and I'd be surprised if anyone seriously accused me of taking it easy on the ice. Hockey is one game in particular where you'd be finished if you did give a halfhearted effort.

Actually, this regular booing of individuals in Chicago was something new in the late 1960s. There had been booing before directed against the whole team, particularly after a poor period, but it hadn't centered on an individual. The players didn't quite know how to react at first, but really couldn't do much other than try to ignore it.

I can't complain, because my overall relationship with the fans has been pretty good. I get a lot of mail and 99% of it contains someone's best wishes. Once in a while kids will give you a laugh, they'll say something like: "I think you're the greatest hockey player in the world. I'd appreciate it if you'd mail me a picture of Pat Stapleton." I try to answer all my fan mail, although sometimes it backs up, and the least I do is send a personally autographed picture.

I guess I got off on the wrong foot with the press when I first broke into the league. I gave short, snappy answers and didn't really talk too much to sportswriters. I've been told it appeared I was uncooperative or stuck-up, although I've always been a man of few words, never realizing it might appear curt. In those days I might tell a writer, "Not now," and let it go at that rather than adding some explanation—that the trainer was waiting to give me some medical attention or that I had out-of-town guests waiting for me. Later on, while I still didn't make speeches, I tried to answer their questions—good or bad—in a little more detail, as well as I could. But for some reason I seemed to get misquoted quite often.

Partly, these misquotations came about because of the very nature of most post-game interviews. You're usually still heated up after a game and quite likely to express yourself a little carelessly, saying something you normally wouldn't when calm and reasonable. You may say things without meaning to and then discover the next day, on picking up the newspaper, that what you said looks bad in print or means something else than what you were trying to say.

Frequently, a writer will walk in on the middle of a conversation between yourself and another writer. He may hear only the second half of your answer to the other writer's question. He'll pick that up and put it in his story. This happens often when you're explaining something first in a positive way, then in a negative. All that gets into the paper is the negative part. My point is that the fault isn't yours, but the sportswriter's, because it's up to him to get the full story. He isn't doing his job.

I can remember an instance in which I was not only completely misrepresented but misquoted to the point that it could have caused serious problems for me. Jim Brosnan, the former baseball pitcher turned writer, wrote an article for Maclean's magazine in Canada. It was one of the worst I ever read.

Regrettably, we all cooperated with him so he could write the story, which was about the Black Hawks. Four or five of us players and a couple of businessmen met him at a restaurant and, as there weren't any tables available, we went to the bar. A couple of the boys had beer, Brosnan ordered a martini, and I asked for a soft drink because that's what I felt like having. Brosnan's story started out something like this: "The fumes from the martini almost got to Mikita because apparently he had had enough the night before so that he didn't want anything to do with the stuff today."

That really put me in a good light! And I didn't even like hard liquor, let alone drink martinis.

The worst part of the story came later. Brosnan and I were talking about the ice at the Chicago Stadium, which was really poor at the time, and I said, "Mr. Wirtz and Mr. Norris don't realize what's going on down there at the Stadium because they don't skate on that ice. If they did go out there and skate they'd know exactly what was wrong with it and I'm sure do something about it."

In Brosnan's article it came out something like: "Norris and Wirtz don't know a darn thing about how the building is run, how the ice is made." In other words, I was represented as having said that my bosses didn't know anything at all about their operation. I was not only misquoted but also made to look like a real ass.

I talked to Mr. Norris about the article and explained to him that Brosnan had misquoted me, and he understood.

"I know what Brosnan's like," he said, "so I'm sure that's not what you said."

It was an incident that could have caused ill feelings, first of all, and maybe even a great deal of harm to my relationship with the management. All through no fault of my own but because of the carelessness and inaccuracy of a writer, who of all people should have known better as he had been a professional athlete himself.

Among the writers who regularly cover the hockey beat in daily American newspapers a problem is that some don't know all the technical aspects of the game that well. Now and then they fail when they try to write as experts, when they try and explain what happened without talking to the coach or players first.

I can understand these writers' problems. Unlike most Canadians, who played hockey as kids, Americans weren't exposed to the game until later in life. They learned as much as they could, but can hardly be expected to know it as well as baseball, which most played as kids. Then, too, the action is so swift it is easy to make mistakes describing a play and maybe they don't have the time afterwards, in the rush of a deadline, to check the facts in the dressing room.

Say a goal is scored. There might be four different reports of how it went into the net, only one of which would be accurate. One writer might say it bounced off a post, another that it went through the goalie's legs, the third that it hit the crossbar, and the fourth that it caught the upper left corner. If you weren't at the game you wouldn't know what happened.

I have no particular quarrel with the columnists, whether they write good or bad things about me, except if they misquote me or obviously fabricate a situation. It's their job to criticize, either to find fault or to praise. That's what they are paid for, and I understand that.

On the other hand writers who cover a game are supposed to be reporters and I think they should stick to that, report what they saw, good or bad, as accurately as possible without trying to analyze things when they aren't completely sure or familiar with what they are writing about.

I'm not saying that it's a reporter's job to cover up for the team, to make it look good when it's stinking out the rink. His first obligation is to his readers. Let him tell the truth. But it's also up to him to find out the truth, not to inject his personal opinions. Some writers always assume when a team gets beaten that it's because the players are lying down on the job or that they're lazy or "racked by dissension," a favorite phrase. The writer could admit that the other team, that night, happened to be better, which is why it won. On any given night, one team, no matter how poor over a season, can be better than any other team, even the best in the league.

I think criticism can be useful if it's based on sound knowledge and judgment. A reporter or a columnist can provide that if he goes to the right people to find out just what is wrong or right about a team or an individual player.

Over all, I can't say my relations with the press have been bad, particularly in recent years. I think I'm even regarded as rather cooperative. There've been a couple of reporters I wouldn't talk to, either because they wrote absolute lies in stories or because they purposely distorted what I said. But in the main I've gotten along well with the press. I know they can help both the club and me and I think they've helped me more than they've hurt me over the years.

I don't quite go along with the well-worn phrase, "You can write anything about me, good or bad, as long as you spell my name right." But it's not far off the mark.

20

Who's No. 2?

THE MAGAZINE article was titled, "The Black Hawks' No. 2 May Make Them No. 1," and when you think about it being considered No. 2 to Bobby Hull's No. 1 isn't exactly a dishonor. Nevertheless, when the writer of the article asked me, "How does it feel to be considered No. 2?" I had to give him an answer straight from the heart.

"Show me a successful man who starts out thinking he's second best in anything, and I doubt he'll ever wind up on top or reach his potential. You have to be positive and think you can do better than somebody else in order to do really well."

It's not an obsession with me to be No. 1 as far as anybody else's evaluation of me in comparison with other hockey players is concerned. It's nice to hear that you're considered better than someone else, but in a way I couldn't care less about how other people rank me—whether they think I'm No. 1, No. 10, or No. 99. I set my sights on becoming No. 1 in the sense of aiming high in whatever I'm doing, giving the very best that's in me. And if somebody says, "You've done a terrific job," that's good, but it doesn't mean as much to me as my own feeling about how well I've done.

It ties in with an overused and sometimes misunderstood word, "desire." To me it means the desire to win a game, because that's the ultimate goal in any athletic contest. If you don't have the desire to win every game you're in then you're just going through the motions. Every effort must be bent toward winning the game. You can go out on the ice and give 100%, but maybe 100% isn't good enough if the desire isn't there. There has to be a goal, the only goal I ever set for myself, and that goal is to win. I'm the worst loser you ever saw because every defeat is a disaster to me at the time. The next day I can think back and console myself with the thought that maybe the other team played better and deserved to win. But I also think that next time we'll play better and we *will* win. The desire also has to be within you to try to do better next time.

Sure, there are nights when you have to push yourself, when you don't feel well physically or ready mentally. That's when you push yourself into a state of wanting to give that 100%. You may only be 80% physically, but then you have to give 100% mentally to get even that 80% out of yourself. If you're well, you should reach your full potential, giving everything you're capable of.

You can't always measure how much you've put out or how close to 100% you get by your goal or point production. I scored four goals in a game against Pittsburgh, and it came on a night when I felt sluggish. I wasn't hurt physically, but I couldn't seem to concentrate on the game as much as I should have before it started. So in that game I had to consciously keep myself up. It just happened that the puck went into the net four times for me. I've played in games in which I felt great mentally and physically and did well in my own estimation without having a point to show for it. Those games were more satisfying to me even than that four-goal game.

It's this quality of desire that creates the outstanding performers. You can take two athletes with equal physical ability and the guy that has more desire is the one who is going to outperform the other—I would want him on my team. You can't always blame a man for having less desire. Some are satisfied with less than other men are. It's just the way they are made up. Maybe their aim is to get fifteen goals a year and they're satisfied with that. Another man is not satisfied with less than thirty goals and his desire to succeed has to be more intense. I don't look at it either way, whether it's fifteen goals or thirty. I don't set any goals for myself in figures, and I'm never satisfied. My goal is to play as hard and as well as I can at all times.

I don't know if the hockey players coming up now have as much desire or less than they did when I first came into the league. I suspect it hasn't changed, that some are hungry and others aren't. From time to time we've had youngsters coming up who looked like world-beaters for three or four days and then dropped out of sight. Then there were kids with less talent, but more desire, who made it. They impressed me more.

One thing for sure: I don't ever want to lose my desire, either to win or to play the game. All I want to do is help in one way or another to win without setting specific personal goals. If my team ended up in first place and I happened to get just ten goals, but I contributed to winning, fine. Maybe my ten goals would be the game-winners or maybe I did a job killing penalties. If my legs and the rest of my body hold out, I'd like to play as long as I can. Not that even that's setting a goal for myself because I go from year to year and I don't look too much into the future in this regard.

Once in a while, I do look into one future, that of hockey in general. And it has to be a bright and changing future, because it's a game on the rise, one that's creating fans among more and more Americans at a rate that's hard to believe.

First all, there's expansion, which certainly hasn't ended. The NHL went to twelve teams in 1967, adding an entire new Western Division of six clubs, all in U.S. cities. And it's almost certain that before long more clubs will be added, with the league going to at least fourteen, maybe even sixteen teams.

I don't think expansion helped or hindered me personally, but others have benefited from it. It gave opportunities to a lot of really good hockey players who had been in the minor leagues to come up and make good salaries by playing in the NHL. And it has extended the careers of a few players who otherwise might have been forced to retire. This is likely to continue during the first ten years of expansion as the supply of good players thins out and until the minor leagues are replenished with experienced and capable men.

Al Arbour, the defenseman who has been such a big help to St. Louis in the last two years, is a fine example of a player who has benefited from expansion. Arbour is one of the best, if not the best, defensive defensemen in the league, and it's a shame that he had to spend so many years in the minors. He doesn't have the best shot in the world but when it comes to defensive play, there's nobody better. To me, defensive skill is what the position of defenseman calls for, and it's really a shame that Arbour didn't get the recognition he deserved until expansion gave him a new chance.

Also it has been proved that a hockey player's useful life on the ice is quite a bit longer than coaches and general managers used to think. There are more men in their late thirties and even early forties playing in the NHL than ever before. And they're doing a good job, which has forced the coaches to a new viewpoint. The older men can play well and also can steady the new, young kids coming up, thus serving a dual purpose for a club.

Expansion also has helped hockey overall, because more people are seeing the game than ever before, both live and on television. As more people are getting enjoyment out of hockey, it also means more money to the owners and the players. The trend is up.

There's another facet of expansion, with teams being located in parts of the United States which at one time knew very little about hockey. Interest is going to produce a new source of player talent, and one of these days a flood of American players is going to enter hockey.

When I first came to the Chicago area there was just one artificial rink available for public use and kids even had to sneak in a shinny game on natural ice before being chased off. In 1969 there were at least seven large artificial rinks within the immediate Chicago area, with more being constructed or planned. And you'll find special ice sections put aside on park lagoons, or flooded rinks with boards constructed just for hockey. Some of the artificial rinks are completely indoors and with ice surfaces not much smaller than those used in the NHL. This increase in rinks gives the youngsters in the Chicago area far more ice time than they were able to get before. But they can't stop there. The youngsters who are playing in the organized leagues must be provided with a chance to continue playing past high school, even if they don't go to college. A system of leagues like the Junior Leagues in Canada is required, and I'm sure it will be set up eventually. If the kids have a chance to play until they are twenty, as they do in Canada, and have the proper training and competition, they'll be coming into the pro leagues before long.

It has been said that American youngsters don't start skating early enough. I really don't think it makes a difference. I've heard of kids starting when they were three and of others who didn't start on skates until they were twelve. Tod Sloan, who was a fine NHL player, didn't start until he was twelve and, at that, he was a figure skater for a while. It's not how late or early you start, but how much effort you put into it and the quality of instruction you get that matters.

While I see hockey expanding and American players coming into it, I also think the game must progress to keep up with the changing times. It's a fast game now, but I think it's going to speed up in the 1970s as it did in the 1960s. It has to if it is to keep the interest and support of the people. In my first ten years in the league the game changed greatly. During my first years it was chiefly a passing game and the wrist shot was dominant. But by the end of the 1960s the momentum had swung to a different kind of game, the slap shot taking over more and more and the pass giving way to dumping the puck into the other team's end and chasing it.

The pace and style of the game are completely different. At one time the only place you could score a goal from was within thirty feet of the net. With the slap shot, goals began to be scored from virtually anywhere on the ice. The people got more action and loved it. It used to be that on the power play the team that was short a man never got a shot on the other team's net. But more and more shorthanded goals began to be scored. Boston won a Stanley Cup game over Montreal in 1969 by scoring two of its three goals while shorthanded.

But as much as the game has been speeded up, I think it will be stepped up even more. People today have turned away from the slower games, like baseball, to such stepped-up games as hockey and football. They don't particularly like to sit around watching nothing happening. They just don't like to sit too long, period. Hockey games run about two hours and fifteen minutes overall. But they could and should be reduced to two hours by cutting out the dead time, the stoppages of play in the game itself. That hour of play should have as little dead time as possible.

I've seen some of the suggestions that have been made to speed up the game, things such as curving the blue lines to reduce the offside calls, reducing the number of face-off circles from five to three, as well as others. I don't know which system would work or whether they would help the game or not, but I think they should be tried out in exhibition games. If they work, fine, put them into the game. If not, you haven't lost a thing.

Take the idea of having three face-off circles instead of five. There would be only one circle in each end zone, directly between the goal and the blue line. It would open up the play immensely, and get rid of the crowding caused by the circles off to one side by the boards.

With the face-off circles by the boards as they are now, the situation is fairly routine. You can almost predict what's going to happen. If the draw goes to the offensive team, the puck gets back to the point man on the board side, he takes a shot, the goalie makes a save and throws the puck into a corner where three or four players pile on it, necessitating another face-off.

If there were just one face-off circle in the end zone, the picture would change. I could draw the puck in either direction and the player who got it would have a darn good shot on net because this way both our wingers could take the other team's wingers out of the play, not interfering with them, but slowing them down enough so they might be a step late in getting out to our pointmen. You would see better shots on net from the point, with an increased chance of scoring. Even when the goalie made a save and threw the puck into a corner there would be less likelihood of congestion and a stoppage of play.

The curved blue lines also would help. This way my winger could be a little ahead of me and I could still give him the puck as I hit the blue line because I would be on side and so would he. The curvature also would make the defenseman back up a little more. Of course, I really don't know if this would make a difference in the long run. It would cut out a lot of offsides at first, but once the players got used to the idea of being so far ahead they would try to get a little farther ahead. It should be tried out in exhibition games, though.

Actually, if a line is working properly there really shouldn't be offsides. What usually causes one is poor control of the puck. Much of the time you don't have good control, but the winger thinks you do so he goes offside.

Another area where some time could be saved would be to force the coaches to change the lines on ice more quickly. There's a lot of jockeying that goes on when there's a face-off. Let coaches be forced to make up their minds right away and have the puck dropped. If they want to make any further changes, let them be made on the fly. The referee should impose a time limit and enforce it, say fifteen or twenty seconds, like the twenty-second rule on pitches they've tried in baseball. I don't think the fans or players like to see the delays. All stalling tactics by coaches should be done away with through proper enforcement of the rules.

Never were these stalling tactics more obvious than in the Stanley Cup semifinals between Boston and Montreal in 1969. Both coaches, Harry Sinden of Boston and Claude Ruel of Montreal, delayed the games numerous times by switching players, trying to gain a slight edge. It was more evident to most people because these games were nationally televised, but our club and others have been just as guilty of this as Boston and Montreal.

Many things have contributed to making the game faster in recent years, including the curved stick. And everybody seems to be looking for a faster game, with people apparently getting bored more quickly than ever. We have to get a step ahead and stay ahead to capitalize on the present intense fan awareness and interest in this game, whether it's by changing the rules or by finding new ways to promote and package it.

Increased American participation in the game is sure to have a great effect both on the promotion of hockey and the way it is played. The promotion changes are already evident in TV and advertising. The effect on the game itself is yet to come, but I'm sure it is on the way. There will be a more scientific analysis of the possibilities of the game by the coaches, and the introduction of aids, such as movie films, video tape replays, and play diagramming, although this is being done to a limited extent now. Not that I think hockey will ever become as thoroughly analyzed or determined as American football. One reason is that, unlike football, a hockey player is not permitted to make body contact with a man who doesn't have the puck. You can't take someone out of a play as easily. So there are limitations on the predetermination of plays. But without doubt, the game will become more scientific and I'm all for it, just as I am for better promotion of hockey.

One of the best ways to promote it has been through television and radio. At one time WGN-TV in Chicago broadcast just a limited number of Hawk road games, but by the late 1960s it carried all away games and now radio station WGN broadcasts the last half of all home games. The influence of TV on kids in the Chicago area was tremendous and Saturday night became almost like hockey night in Canada. The kids and adults turned on the TV and waited for the announcer to say, "Hello, hockey fans, this is Lloyd Pettit from the Forum in Montreal."

You could see the kids' interest in hockey grow from what it had been. Years before it was an oddity when you saw a kid walking down the street with a hockey stick over his shoulder and carrying a pair of skates. But by 1969 everybody seemed to be carrying skates and sticks, and you could see the youngsters playing road hockey, something unheard of before. And I think it was all because of that one-eyed monster.

My mail reflected the growth in interest. About 60% of the letters I got from kids started out with a request for a tip on how to take a face-off, how to stick-handle, how to get off a slap shot, and only as an afterthought did the youngster ask for a picture or an autograph.

I don't have to have a crystal ball to predict how all these things are going to change hockey, and I'm not one of those guys who is worried that the changes won't be for the better.

Take expansion, which a lot of people feared would lower the quality of play and dilute the talent to the point where the whole league would be hurt. As far as I could see, there was no drop in the quality of the game, just a change in the way it was played.

Maybe somebody that has been watching the game for thirty years would say, "Well, these kids coming up now aren't as good as the kids we had coming up thirty years ago." I don't know, since I wasn't around thirty years ago, but when you see a team do as well against all opposition as St. Louis did in its first two years in the NHL you wonder what these people are talking about. Then there was Oakland, with a bunch of youngsters on its team, which took five out of six games from the Black Hawks in the 1968–69 season. There was nothing wrong with the quality of their play.

It seems to me that as expansion continued the talent became so well distributed that any team might beat any other team on a given night. The universal draft of players that the NHL has put into effect will continue to spread that talent evenly and the management of each club will have to show it knows how to make the right selections.

No, I can't be worried about the future of hockey, as long as the supply of talent keeps growing and as long as the game keeps pace with the times. The fan support is there, and I think hockey interests in the U.S. will continue to spread and grow by leaps and bounds.

For myself, the future doesn't frighten me any more than the past has. And all the trophies I won in the first ten years didn't affect me as much as people might think. As I mentioned before, maybe the first year after I stop playing I'll sit back and say, "Gee, that was really nice, getting all that silverware," and get real satisfaction out of looking at it.

Who's No. 2?

But you really don't know what you have accomplished until you're finished with the game and people start comparing you with the young kids playing then. They might say, "Well, who is better, this kid or Mikita when he was playing?" And if the kid whom they're comparing you with is great you might think, "Gee, maybe I was pretty good if I played like this fellow does." Or if the kid isn't too good, you'd say to yourself, "I played that way? I guess I wasn't much good."

When you're still playing you don't like to say or think—really can't do so—that you've reached your peak or the pinnacle of achievement. It goes back to what you're satisfied with, what you'll settle for. If you're satisfied with ninety-seven points in a season, fine. If you're satisfied with a hundred, that's fine too. If you're satisfied to end up in last place, as the Black Hawks did in 1968–69, that may be fine for some, but not me. And I was never satisfied with ninety-seven points, I don't think I would be with a hundred or any figure you might name. There's no such thing as satisfaction in my case, because I always want to do better.

It would be nice to have your team end up in first place and then take the Stanley Cup, but that's only for one year and the next year you have to go out and prove yourself again. In fact, you want to prove yourself again . . . and again . . . and again. It's like getting stuck in a revolving door. You're always reaching for something in the hope that you can grab it. You seldom do, but all the fun is in the trying.

It's like that in life and in hockey. If you play to win, as I do, the game never ends.